A Mouthpiece Buzzing Routine for Trumpet

Lynn K. Asper

First Edition

WaveSong Press

Hudsonville, Michigan

1138 Fairfield Dr.
Hudsonville, MI 49426
(616) 457- 0562

Library of Congress Catalog Card Number on File.

ISBN 0-9668847-0-X

Editor: Renée Dunnette Asper

Printed in the United States of America

This book is dedicated to Boyde Hood, who has inspired me in so many ways.

Table of Contents

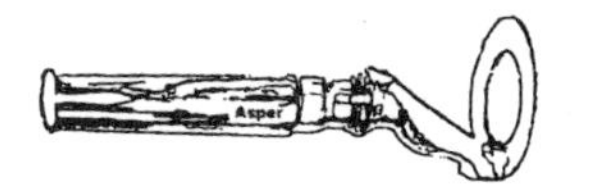

Table of Figures

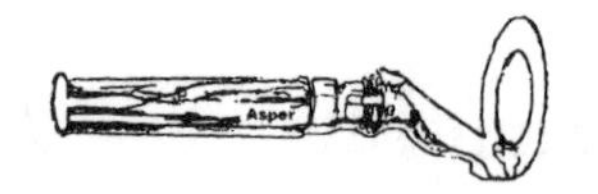

Appendices

Preface

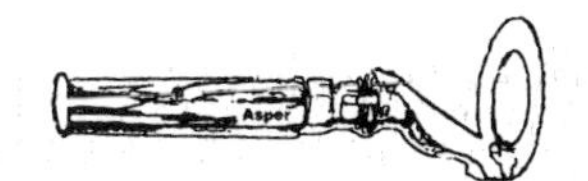

A Mouthpiece Buzzing Routine Based Upon Physical Techniques

This book exploring the mouthpiece buzzing routine is an expansion of the trumpet mouthpiece buzzing routine that appears in my book A Physical Approach to Playing the Trumpet. Since that book was published in 1999, I have expanded my ideas on the topic of mouthpiece buzzing.

A Physical Approach to Playing the Trumpet is based partly upon my belief that, when a part of the body involved in playing the trumpet is not responding properly, change rarely occurs through listening to more literature or 'playing through the problem'. My experience tells me that the body will likely *not* correct itself. Sadly, I have seen too many players practice incorrect habits waiting for a day that will never arrive!

My physical approach attempts to avoid intangible concepts by explaining the physical skill to be applied to each area of playing so that the player can learn the *correct physical response* for every playing situation. Tangible, concrete, and logical, this method can be taught in a step-by-step manner which players find easy to understand and apply.

The physical approach to playing the trumpet is a proactive way to identify barriers to playing improvement and apply specific techniques to overcome those barriers. It is based upon the science of body mechanics, making it possible for the player to see and feel changes as they occur. The player has immediate feedback and does not lose precious time that might have been devoted to practicing bad habits.

Why Write a Book on Mouthpiece Buzzing?

During the summer of 2002, I had several conversations with my former trumpet teacher, Boyde Hood, during which he shared his ideas on the subject of mouthpiece buzzing. When I was studying with him in the late 1960's, we did not do a lot of mouthpiece buzzing. However, in the last several years I have been doing more in this area. During my recent discussions with Boyde, I discovered that he, too, has begun to do more in this area.

During those conversations we discovered that we had both adopted a more comprehensive mouthpiece buzzing routine. Boyde shared his ideas on the subject as well as some of the ideas used by his former teacher, Adolph 'Bud' Herseth. We had, in the intervening 33 years, come to many of the same conclusions about the use of mouthpiece buzzing in the daily warm-up.

How This Book is Organized

This book was written for intermediate to advanced trumpet players and their teachers. You will notice that the book is written in a first person, question-and-answer format. I have found that I can anticipate many of the questions that players tend to ask about mouthpiece buzzing. Writing in this conversational format simply seems natural to me.

This book is most effective when a teacher uses it with a student. The teacher then becomes an embouchure analyst. Over time and with practice, the player should become better and better at analyzing their own embouchure, so barriers can be overcome through the use of this book and the techniques described – even when a teacher is not immediately available.

The first section of the book is devoted to defining the technical aspects of mouthpiece buzzing. Figures and photographs are used to reinforce the written descriptions. However, knowing *what* to play during buzz practice is as important as knowing *how* to buzz. For this purpose, daily buzzing routines are also covered.

Specific musical examples are located in the Appendices. Various units throughout the book will explain how to use these exercises. Grouping the musical exercises together at the end of the book will eventually make them easier to locate and use during practice. Once the player understands the intent of each exercise, they will not need to flip back and forth through the book to find an exercise.

In my many years as an educator, I have discovered that each player I meet has also had something to teach me. This connection has been very important to me and I realize that teaching via a book does not allow for this type of interaction. I would welcome your communication at wavesong@att.net or (616) 457-0562. My address is Mr. Lynn K. Asper, Trumpet Studio, 1138 Fairfield Dr., Hudsonville MI, 49426.

About the Author

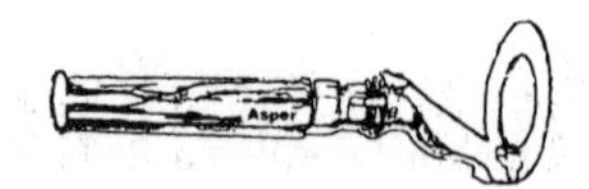

Lynn K. Asper is a native of South Bend, Indiana. He holds a Bachelor of Science in Music Education Degree from Ball State University and a Master of Music Education Degree from Michigan State University. With a father, Franklin Asper, who played the trumpet, and a trumpet-playing older brother, Norman Asper, it was destiny that Lynn would become a trumpet player and teacher.

Robert Ralston, Lynn's beginning band teacher in South Bend, was also his first official trumpet teacher. By the ninth grade, Lynn was studying with Jay Miller (ret.), a graduate of Indiana University and a student of Bill Adam. During his undergraduate years at Ball State University Lynn studied with Max Woodbury, who was then a member of the Indianapolis Symphony Orchestra, and Boyde Hood, the trumpet instructor at Ball State University. Lynn considers Boyde to have had the greatest impact upon his trumpet playing. Boyde had studied with Adolf 'Bud' Herseth, principal trumpet with the Chicago Symphony Orchestra (ret.). In graduate school at Michigan State University, Lynn studied with Byron Autrey (ret.).

Lynn K. Asper spent ten years teaching high school music at Ottawa Hills High School in Grand Rapids, Michigan. He was asked to join the music faculty at Grand Rapids Community College in 1979, and remained there as a full-time teacher until 2002. Lynn continues teaching part-time as professor of trumpet, conductor of the trumpet ensemble, and conductor of the Kent Philharmonia Orchestra. He is also active as a clinician for Edwards Trumpets, a distributor for Warburton trumpet mouthpieces, and is the builder and distributor of the Asper Trumpet Mouthpiece Visualizer. As a trumpet player, Mr. Asper performs with the music ministry at Fair Haven Ministries, the Kent Brass, the Grand River Big Band and the A.T.A.R. Trio. His trumpet method book, A Physical Approach to Playing the Trumpet, is currently in its third printing and has proven to be a valuable asset in trumpet playing and teaching communities all over the world.

Acknowledgements

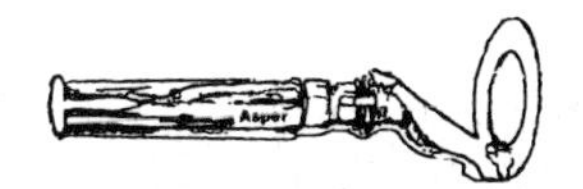

I would like to acknowledge the following people who helped make this book possible.

- All of the trumpet students who have passed through Grand Rapids Community College;
- To our models; Renée Asper, Jeff Ayres, Ernie Bader, Steve Bookshaw, Randy Flynn, Lois Gerke, Lisa Kacos, Kris McKay, and Mark Sluiter;
- My wife Renée; editor, photographer and supporter;
- Kris McKay, Edie Dunnette Lampen, Jeff Ayres, Mark Sluiter, Mike Truszkowski, Wayne Rosebery, and Kevin Dobreff who helped me edit drafts;
- Dr. I. Edward Alcamo, Ph.D. and Random House, Inc. for the use of the muscle drawings originally produced for Anatomy Coloring Workbook;
- Paul Bultinck and Will Murphy from Grand Rapids **METALTEK** Inc., for their help in the design and manufacture of the **Asper Trumpet Mouthpiece Visualizer.**

Unit 1 Introduction

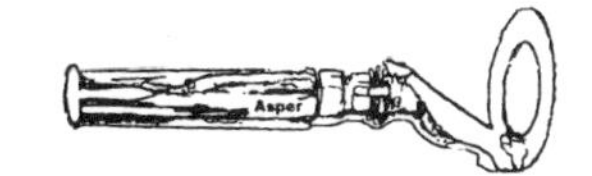

Why did you write this book?

Many trumpet players use a mouthpiece buzzing routine as part of their daily warm-up. In my conversations with Boyde Hood, we agreed that as trumpet players who play every day, the 'what we do' in the daily warm-up is more about *yesterday's* playing than the playing we're planning to do today. This assumes that playing is done on a daily basis. Most trumpet players tend to end each day with some kind of fatigue. Many times this fatigue is experienced the next morning as a feeling of puffiness or swelling of the muscles and flesh in the embouchure. The length of time we play each day seems to control how long it takes to warm-up the next morning. More playing equals more impact upon the embouchure. When I feel puffy or swollen in the morning, it is beneficial for my embouchure to <u>not</u> begin the practice routine on the trumpet itself. Something else needs to be done first.

In an attempt to discover the best way to overcome this fatigue, I began using the James Stamp mouthpiece buzzing exercises. They are well respected and I found that they were very beneficial to me. These routines helped me concentrate on the condition of the embouchure, how it looked, and how it responded – all without having the weight of the trumpet on my face. For me, however, the trumpet mouthpiece buzzing alone would take quite a long time each morning. If I had played a three set big band performance the night before, it might have taken up to an hour to recover. I had a feeling that I was missing something. I needed to find a method that would enable me to warm-up both efficiently and properly, even if I had played heavily the day before.

In further conversations with Boyde, he suggested that I try two things prior to playing the James Stamp buzzing routine:

1. Start the mouthpiece buzzing routine on a mouthpiece that has a rim size that is *larger* than a trumpet mouthpiece.
2. After buzzing on a large mouthpiece, continue the buzzing routine on a mouthpiece *visualizer* before going to the trumpet mouthpiece.

These suggestions led me to develop a mouthpiece buzzing routine that addressed all the issues I was dealing with. This is the method I will share with you in this book.

Unit 2 Equipment

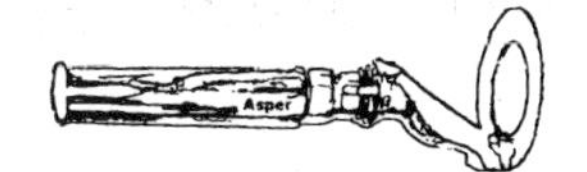

OK, so what do I need?

You will need 3 things:

- A big mouthpiece
- A trumpet mouthpiece visualizer
- Your trumpet mouthpiece

What big mouthpiece should I use?

Boyde Hood tells a story about a lesson with Bud Herseth. After the lesson was over, Bud stated that his embouchure felt 'tight' and that he was going to go back and do some *alto horn* mouthpiece buzzing. Boyde had heard of large mouthpiece buzzing before but did not know that Bud was using the technique. Bud said that there were really two benefits from buzzing on the alto horn mouthpiece. First, you must take in a tremendous amount of air to buzz on a rim size that large, and, secondly, the buzz that results is very wide open and *relaxed.*

I believe that this relaxed buzz is what helps swollen lips recover quickly.

Would a trombone or euphonium mouthpiece work just as well?

I do not believe they would for two reasons. First, the mouthpiece rim size must be larger than the largest trumpet mouthpiece rim size, but not so large that the embouchure used in buzzing on the big mouthpiece is not 'trumpet like' in the way it feels. Secondly, using the alto horn rim size *allows us to see embouchure symmetry* very much like the trumpet embouchure's symmetry. What we need is a mouthpiece rim size which is somewhere between the largest trumpet mouthpiece and the smallest trombone mouthpiece. Result – *the alto horn mouthpiece!*

What size alto horn mouthpiece should I use, and where can I get one?

Most of the players I have worked with find that the Bach 3 alto horn mouthpiece works very well. Once in a while I may see a player with *very* small, thin lips. In that case I may have the player try a Bach 5 alto horn mouthpiece. Most of the time, however, the Bach 3 alto horn mouthpiece does the job. I will give more detail in Unit 11 concerning this issue.

You should be able to find the Bach 3 alto horn mouthpiece in most large music stores. However, they are sometimes out of stock and ordering one through a small music store may take a long time. The fastest way to get one is through WaveSong Press at www.trumpetbook.com or simply use the order form on page 95.

Earlier you used the phrase 'embouchure symmetry'. How does this work?

The entire mouthpiece buzzing routine must be done in front of a mirror!!

I also believe that it is very beneficial to continue to stay in front of the mirror through the first part of the warm-up on the trumpet. (I will describe mirror practice in more detail in Units 11, 12 and 13.)

Embouchure symmetry refers to the shape of the muscle structure and the amount of firmness or relaxation that occurs on each side of the mouthpiece. We should see the same amount of firmness on each side. If we were to use a mouthpiece that is *much* larger than a trumpet mouthpiece, the amount of firmness would be quite different than the trumpet mouthpiece. The use of the alto horn mouthpiece, although bigger, is close enough in rim size to allow the player to hold the embouchure in much the same way as if using a trumpet mouthpiece, yet you can still begin the mouthpiece buzzing routine with greater relaxation of the buzz. (Compare the embouchure symmetry in Figures 9 and 37.)

Is there any other benefit to buzzing on the alto horn mouthpiece?

Yes. It gives you some time to engage your brain and make a connection to your body to prepare for the trumpet work of the day. To 'engage the brain', you must rid your mind of all thoughts that are not related to trumpet playing. When you are able to begin your warm-up with a clear head, then you are able to pay attention to the information, or signals, that your body is sending to your brain. This is sometimes difficult to do, given the hectic pace of our lives and the many non-musical responsibilities we have. Like everything else, engaging your brain and tuning in to your body takes practice.

What is a trumpet mouthpiece visualizer?

A mouthpiece visualizer is designed to allow a player to see their lips inside the mouthpiece rim. The older style trumpet mouthpiece visualizers were made of metal and shaped like a trumpet mouthpiece rim but not made from a real trumpet mouthpiece. This rim usually had some kind of handle or tapered shank on it so as to simulate a trumpet mouthpiece. The mouthpiece cup didn't exist so that the player could see their lips inside the rim. This style of trumpet mouthpiece visualizer is still around and has been for a very long time. During the late 1960's, this was what we used because it was all that was available.

Figure 1 Visualizer with handle

Did this type of visualizer work well for you?

No. For me there were actually two problems. It didn't seem to matter how I held this 'visualizer with a handle', I could not achieve the proper weight distribution of the rim on my embouchure. It seemed that the angle of the handle made proper weight distribution impossible. No matter what I did, it did not feel like a trumpet mouthpiece.

Figure 2

Visualizer with handle to the side

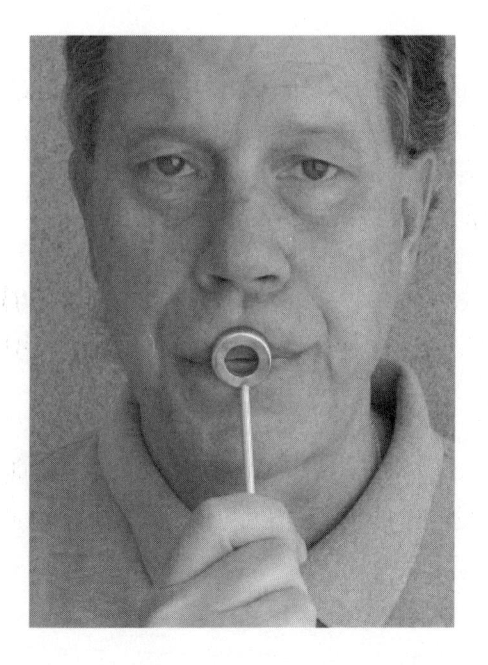

Figure 3

Visualizer with handle downward

The second problem was that this visualizer with a handle was only manufactured in one rim size (approximately a 3C). I was playing on a 1¼ rim size at the time. Nothing felt right using the '3C' visualizer. I soon stopped using it as a part of any routine.

Has the mouthpiece rim size issue been resolved in the past 30 years?

Not to my satisfaction. However, there are several mouthpiece manufacturers who are building trumpet mouthpiece visualizers.

The 'rim on a stick' is still available and there is a company building a '3' rim size that is soldered to a tapered shank using two small metal rods. The tapered shank then fits into the trumpet. (Only a '3' rim size is available.)

The other mouthpiece manufacturers who produce mouthpiece visualizers make them out of trumpet mouthpieces that, during routine production, fail the size tolerance testing process. These mouthpieces are then retooled into visualizers. Due to the modern, computer driven manufacturing process, these companies only have 15-25 mouthpieces *a year* that fail. This means that there are not many visualizers available that are made from real trumpet mouthpieces, and the ones that *do* exist are not available in predictable sizes.

Nearly any mouthpiece company will cut a mouthpiece visualizer out of a real mouthpiece that has passed the size tolerance testing process, but this can get very expensive and there is a very long waiting period for delivery. Most companies have very few in stock.

So where can I get a trumpet mouthpiece visualizer that is a real trumpet mouthpiece and still order it by rim size at a reasonable price?

I'm glad you asked that question! You know the old adage that says; "If you look for a product on the market that you really need but can't find, build it yourself."

So I did!

Introducing

The Asper Trumpet Mouthpiece Visualizer!

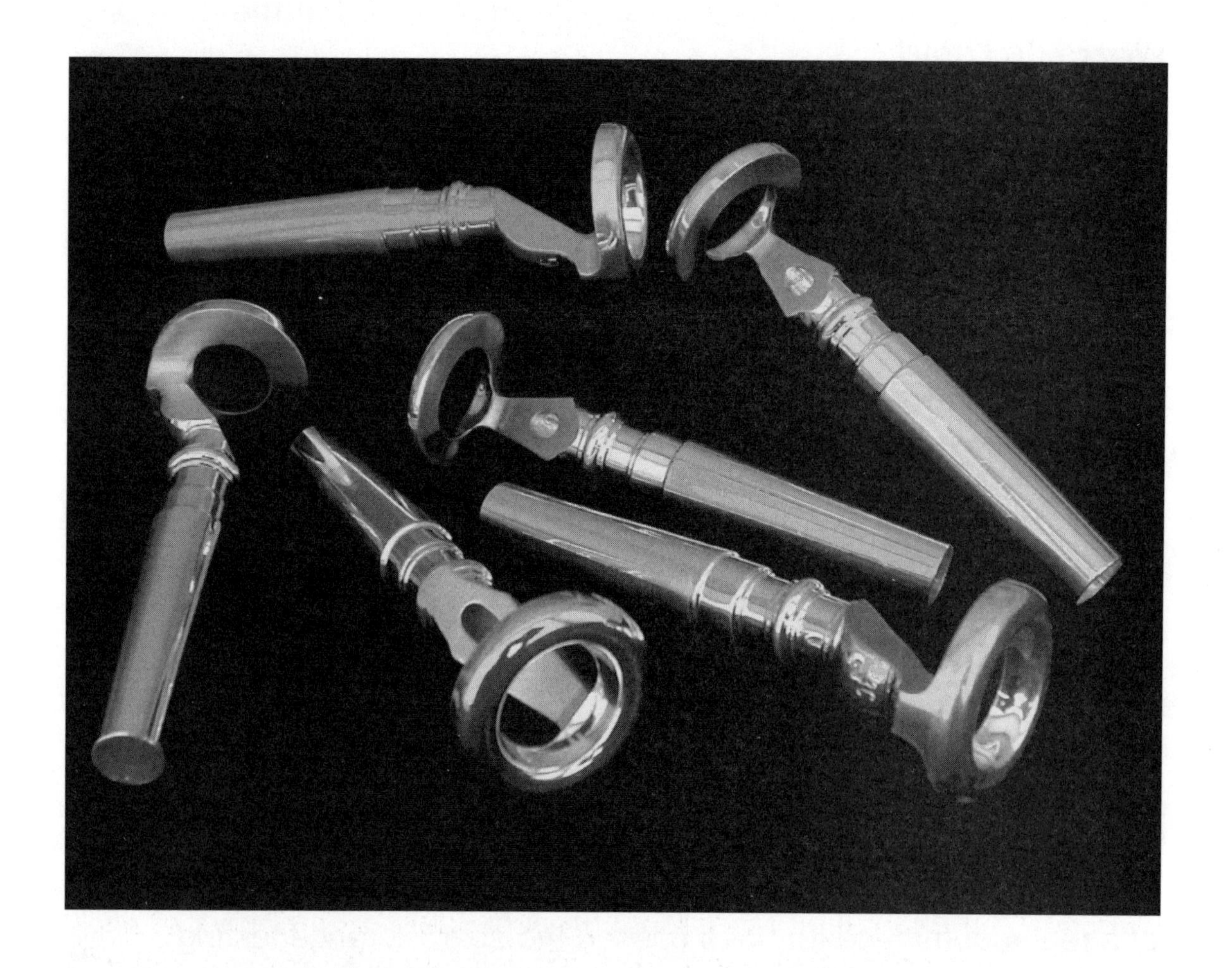

Size really does matter!

Available in sizes:
1C, 1¼C, 1½C, 3C, 5C, 7C, 10½C

See page 91 for ordering details!

Unit 3 The Basics

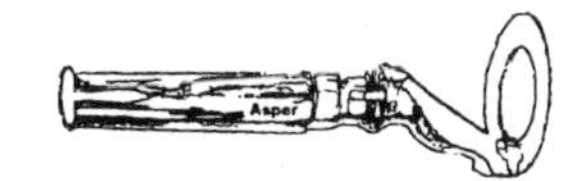

Where do I start?

Let's start by looking at three of the underlying groups of reflexes that are used in trumpet playing and trumpet mouthpiece buzzing: the air column (including the air intake system), the embouchure, and the buzz pitch. Understanding these concepts will help you maximize the benefits of the buzzing routine. So, a little background first.

What is the air column and how is it used to play the trumpet or mouthpiece?

Air column is the process of gathering air into the body and properly using it to play the trumpet. It is easiest to grasp this concept by following along with the experiment described below.

Let's do an experiment. Visualize two tubes. The tubes are identical except for the fact that one is larger in diameter. At one end of each tube there are identical air compressors, and at the opposite end of each tube there are identical air-speed indicators.

Question: If each air compressor can push identical amounts of air at identical speeds, *through which tube will the air move faster?*

Answer: The tube with the smaller diameter.

Now let's envision suspending an identical piece of material hanging down in each tube, and blow air against them.

Question: Will the pieces of material vibrate?

Answer: Yes, when the air goes fast enough.

Question: When the pieces of identical vibrating material vibrate, will they each produce a pitch?

Answer: Yes.

Question: When the pieces of vibrating material in each tube have identical volumes of air flowing against them (creating a pitch), will the pitches be the same?

Answer: No, the piece of vibrating material in the smaller tube will vibrate at a higher pitch than the piece in the larger tube.

Let's suspend another piece of vibrating material in each tube. Now each tube has two pieces of material vibrating inside it.

Question: The first piece of vibrating material we put in each tube was rather thin. The second piece of vibrating material we put in each tube was rather thick. As we send air through each tube, will the two pieces of vibrating material vibrate at the same pitch?

Answer: No. The thin piece of material will vibrate at a higher pitch than the thick one.

The two pieces of material, although vibrating independently, contribute to an overall sound produced in the tube. Let's say that the sound produced can be measured upon a scale from 'dark, warm, open and wide' to 'bright, cold, focused and narrow'.

Question: If we could control which piece of vibrating material contributes more to the sound, and we chose the thin piece, where on our 'dark versus bright' scale would the resulting sound be located?

Answer: The sound would be more on the 'bright, cold, focused and narrow' end of the scale.

Question: If we could get the thick piece of vibrating material to contribute more to the sound, then where on the scale would the resultant sound be located?

Answer: The sound would be more on the 'warm, dark, open and wide' end of the scale.

What does this experiment have to do with trumpet playing or mouthpiece buzzing?

Our lungs and abdominal muscles are the air compressors, our trachea is the tube, the upper lip is the thin piece of vibrating material, and the lower lip is the thick piece of vibrating material (allowing some leeway for embouchure structure to be slightly different from human to human).

How do I vary the diameter of the tube (trachea)?

There are two ways to do this. The first way is to raise and lower the tongue in the mouth by forming the vowel shapes: 'oh', 'ah', 'eh', 'ih', and 'ee'. Moving from one vowel shape to another will change the speed of the air *as it passes through the mouth,* without changing the size of the air tube, or trachea.

Note: Faster Air = Higher Pitch

The second way to vary the diameter of the tube is by closing the throat, or trachea. (I will refer to the trachea as the throat for the remainder of this book. Although not anatomically precise, I believe it is easier to understand for our purposes.) I do not recommend the throat-closing technique until the player is quite advanced. Once the throat closes for any reason, it tends not to open back up all of the way. We must almost always play with an open throat to use our air efficiently.

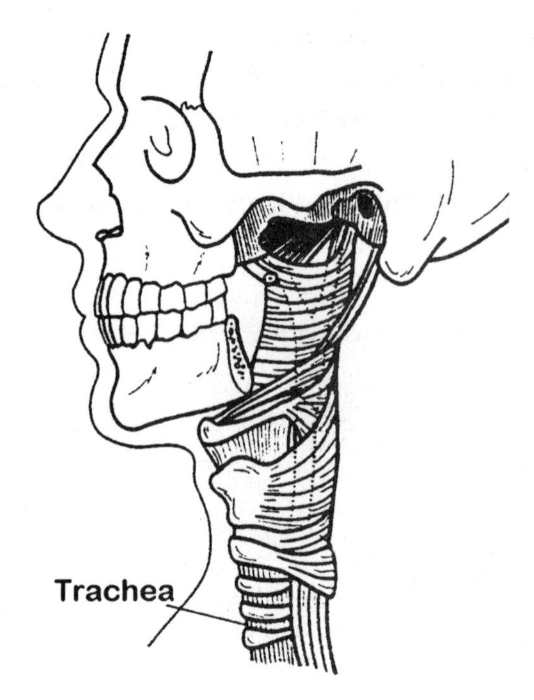

Figure 5 The Trachea

What happens if I just blow harder? Doesn't that speed up the air?

Yes, it does to a certain extent. However, blowing more air also produces a louder sound. Many young players discover this and never learn any other method for playing in the upper register. This is mostly why many trumpet players can only play in the upper register at a loud volume. If the music calls for a high note at a soft volume, the player who uses this technique exclusively is stuck.

I know that I need to take a big breath to play the trumpet or trumpet mouthpiece, but how do I know if I'm taking in enough air?

Many players do not know what a big breath feels like. Your body may never have experienced a full, deep breath and has no frame of reference. We all *think* we can take in a big breath when we, for example, try to blow up an inflatable toy.

So let's try another experiment. Go to the local hardware store and buy yourself a plastic ¾" insert coupling (look near the 'do it yourself' underground sprinkling department). ¾" is the exterior measurement. It will cost about 50¢. The insert coupling is made of plastic and is used to attach two pieces of pipe internally. Be sure it is ¾" and not ½". The ¾" tube is just about the size of the opening around the trumpet mouthpiece when it's on your embouchure.

Figure 6

¾ inch insert coupling

Clean the tube well, then place about half of the tube in your mouth, sealing your lips around it. Put your tongue in the bottom of your mouth like you're saying 'ho', and breathe in. *That's what a deep breath feels like.* If this feeling is new to you, you should do this exercise several times at the beginning of your practice session. Your body will, over time, learn to recognize this as the feeling it should experience when a deep breath is required. After a while, you'll only need to use the tube occasionally for reinforcement.

Figure 7

'HO' breath with the tube

Unit 4 Embouchure

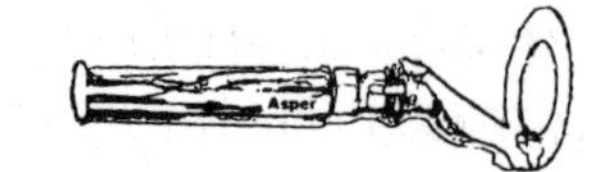

What is the proper embouchure?

em·bou·chure \am-bu-shu(e)r\ n. 1: the position and use of the lips in producing a musical tone on a wind instrument

Consistent with the other reflex group we have studied, the proper embouchure is as efficient as possible. As you can see from Figure 8, there is a muscle called the orbicularis oris that is in the shape of an oval ring surrounding the opening of the mouth. This muscle forms the support for the embouchure. The strength of this muscle is directly related to the endurance and flexibility required to play in all ranges. Developing this muscle through disciplined practice will increase the amount of muscle that can be placed under the mouthpiece rim, which increases the amount of vibration that can be achieved. Play on muscle!

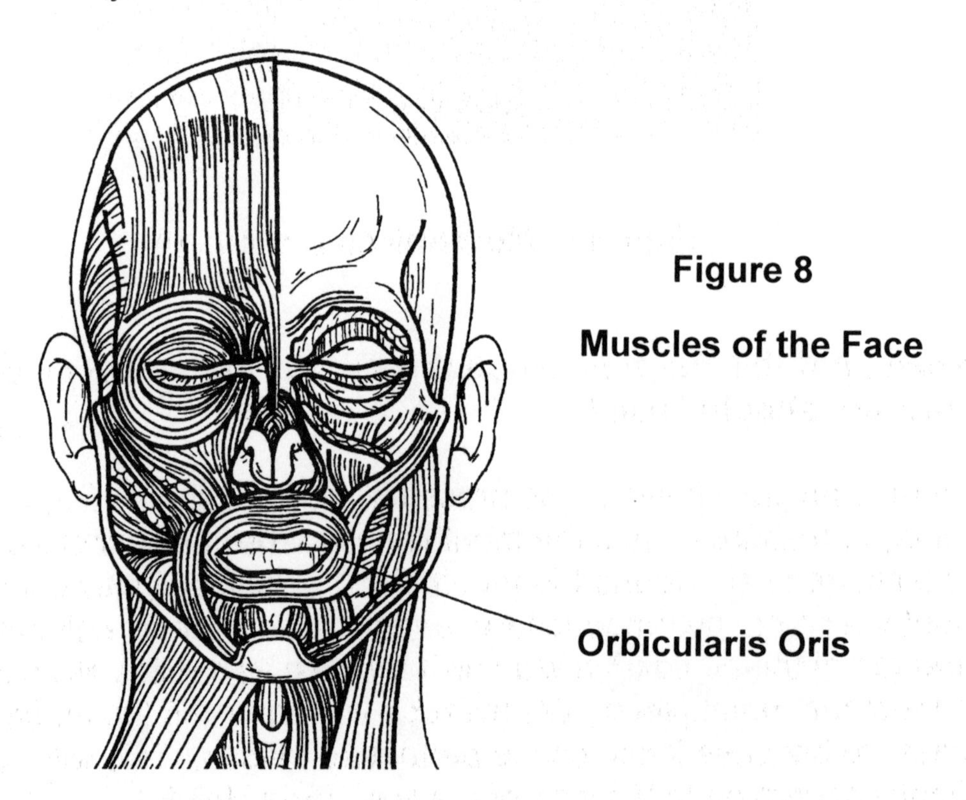

Figure 8

Muscles of the Face

When forming the trumpet embouchure, the lips may need to be rolled in slightly while being held firm at the corners. (This may be altered slightly if the player has fleshy lips. I will go into more detail in Unit 8 when we talk about the shape of the face and lips.) The mouthpiece must be placed on the lips so as to allow as much upper lip to vibrate *inside the mouthpiece/visualizer* as possible (given the size of the lips). This lip formation should closely resemble the shape of the orbicularis oris muscle structure and should be held quite firmly for most playing. When the trumpet player experiences fatigue, it should be in the area of the muscle structure of the face, *not the flesh where the mouthpiece/visualizer contacts the lips.*

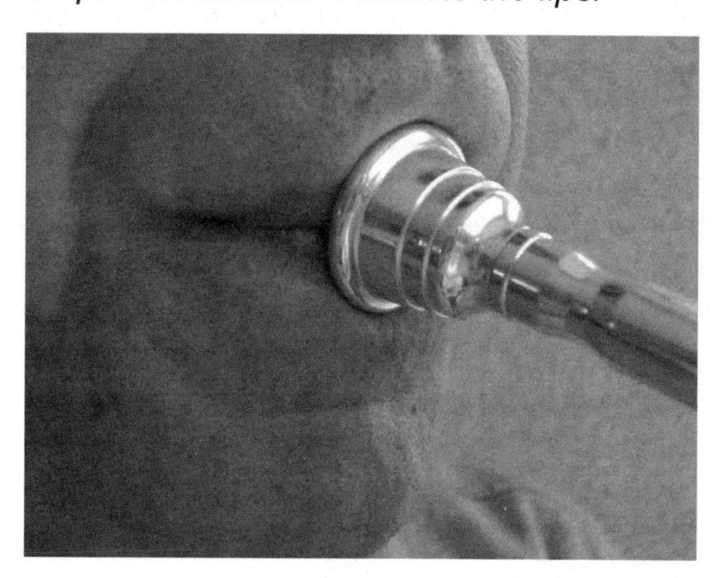

Figure 9 Mouthpiece placement

When I put the mouthpiece on the embouchure, how much pressure should I use?

There is no such thing as 'no pressure', but you should use just enough pressure to seal the mouthpiece to the lips so there can be no leakage of air around the mouthpiece. Think of lightly placing the mouthpiece on the embouchure, and then blow the air column. The strength of the air column will finish the seal as the lips are blown out to meet the mouthpiece. We must be wary of using too much pressure because it can cause premature fatigue. This will vary slightly according to the size of the lips. (See Unit 8.)

Should the weight of the horn be the same on each lip?

Most of the time you will play with of the weight of the horn on the lower lip. We will alter this slightly when playing in the low register or pedal range.

How will I alter this?

In order to understand the relationship of mouthpiece placement to playing in various ranges we need to define three key words: anchor, buzz, and pivot.

Even though we would like to use only as much pressure as is necessary for a good seal, the weight of the horn or mouthpiece has to be someplace to get a complete seal of the mouthpiece/visualizer on the embouchure. We need to determine where to place the mouthpiece in order to maximize lip vibration to efficiently produce the sound we want on the trumpet or any of the mouthpieces.

For example, if we want to play a mid-range to high note, we want to have as much upper lip vibration as possible. We would put the weight of the horn on the bottom lip. The actual placement of the weight of the horn on the lips is called the anchor. If we need to play a low to pedal-range note, the bottom lip could help us by vibrating a little more, so we could put some weight on the upper lip. If we needed to play a note in the middle register, the weight of the horn would be fairly equal on both lips, or stay on the bottom lip. We'll actually move the anchor from one lip to the other while we are going from the upper register to the lower, or vise versa. This horn or mouthpiece weight movement is called the pivot. Notice that I have intentionally used the word 'weight' not 'pressure'.

Sometimes I change my embouchure from playing in the upper register to playing in the lower register. Is this ok?

Many players do change embouchures when moving from register to register. I do not recommend this; *it's inefficient* If the literature calls for you to leap huge intervals, the embouchure change will not happen fast enough. I prefer using and teaching the pivot method described above.

How are the anchor and the buzz related?

The buzz is actually the sound that the lips make inside the mouthpiece cup or visualizer rim. They make this sound *vibrating separately*. Although the lips come close to each other inside the mouthpiece, they are independent vibrators. The anchor is the placement of the mouthpiece weight on the lips and affects which lip vibrates more. By changing the position of the anchor, you change the amount of vibration that is possible for each lip.

There have been some recent laboratory experiments which indicate that the upper lip does most of the vibrating during the buzz, and that the lower lip only vibrates sympathetically. Most of the time, trumpet players are called upon to play in the middle to upper register of their instrument. This means that much of the time the anchor will be placed on the bottom lip allowing the upper lip to do the vibrating. I believe that, although the lower lip doesn't vibrate nearly as much as the upper lip does in the buzz, placement of the anchor slightly on the upper lip will allow the lower lip to vibrate sufficiently to open up the lower register of the trumpet or the mouthpiece/visualizer, especially in the pedal range of the trumpet. This will make the trumpet sound wider. Remember, this only works if you do not put too much weight on the top lip.

What is the relationship among the anchor, the buzz, and the pivot?

Actually, both the anchor and pivot affect the buzz. Remember, the pivot is the movement of the anchor from the bottom lip to the top, such as would be necessary to play an arpeggio starting on a low note. Having the anchor placed on the bottom lip most of the time will allow the top lip to vibrate more freely. When the top lip vibrates freely, the tone quality becomes wider and more open. When the upper lip is pinned down by mouthpiece weight, especially when playing in the middle to upper register, the resulting tone quality will be pinched, thin, fuzzy, unfocused and narrow. When learning the pivot initially, you will move the horn or mouthpiece substantially. As your body understands what the pivot is, the movement will become a subtle combination of horn, jaw, and embouchure movement.

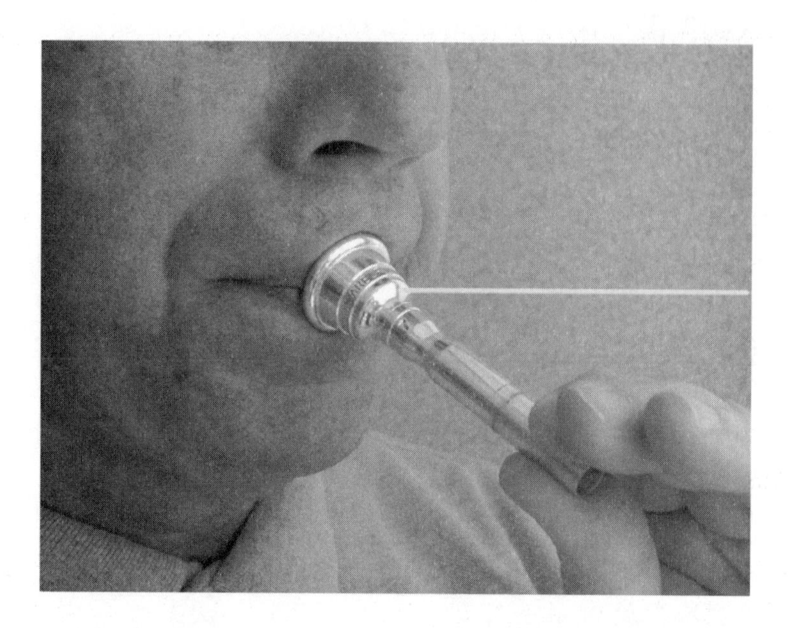

Figure 10 Pivot for the middle to upper register

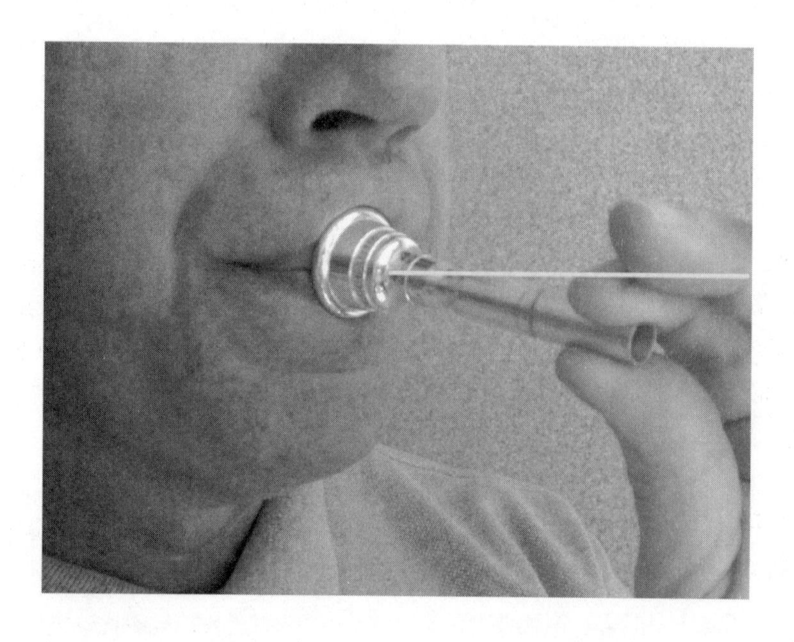

Figure 11 Pivot for the low register

Unit 5 Air Intake

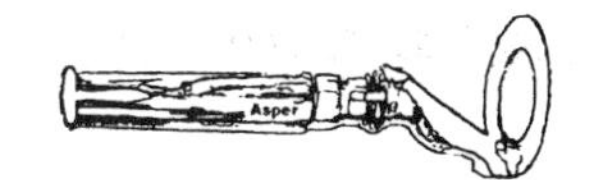

What is air intake?

In Unit 3, The Basics, we discussed the movement of air, the speed of air and its relationship to pitch, and what it really feels like to take a big breath. This unit will help you apply these concepts by discussing the air intake reflex group.

Now that I know what a deep breath feels like, should I always breathe this way?

Yes. We should always take a full, deep breath. This process is referred to as air intake. The amount of air we take in should *not* be affected by length of phrase, dynamic level marked, or any other factor. *Take in maximum air all of the time!* When taking air in, you must form the vowel 'ho' and breathe in just as you did with the 'tube' in your mouth (Figure 7). I called this taking a 'ho' breath and even have a special breath mark I use to remind myself to breathe this way when marking literature – °.

I would like to make one last point about air intake or full, deep breathing. For some reason, we tend to take air in during the one *beat* prior to our next entrance. If the tempo is 80 beats per minute or faster, this does not allow us enough time to take a full, deep breath. I would prefer that you take one full *second* to breathe, no matter how fast the music is marked. This may seem awkward at first and does take a lot of practice. It is well worth your effort.

If I take a full, deep breath all the time, won't I almost always have more air than I need?

Yes, but this is a *good* thing. How many times have you been told to "play with breath support", or "you need to support your sound". Did anyone ever tell you what breath support really is? Breath support is *air in reserve*. This can best be achieved by striving to perfect the air intake mechanism so that it is consistently helping you fill to capacity with air.

Might I spend as much time exhaling as I do inhaling?

When you are playing on the trumpet the answer is "yes". When you are buzzing on the visualizer/mouthpieces, you will use all of your air during each exercise.

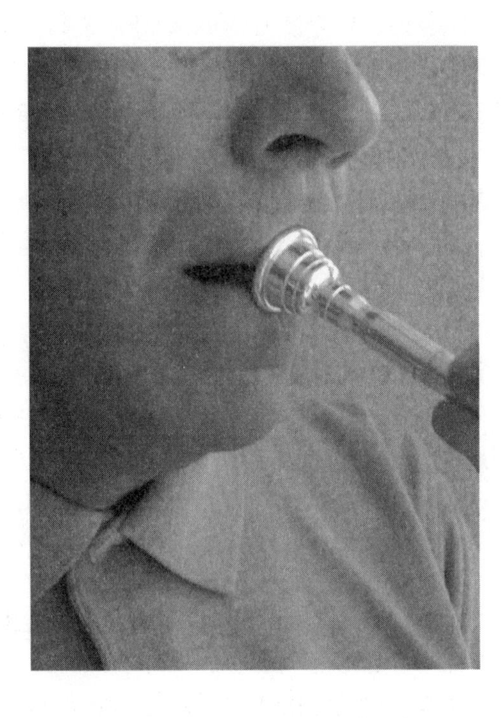

Figure 12

The 'HO' breath

Many players find it helpful to place their right hand on their stomach just above their belt buckle during the air intake. This helps the player concentrate on the feeling of the air intake and the grip of firmness of the oblique muscles as the blowing mechanism begins.

Unit 6 Buzz Pitch

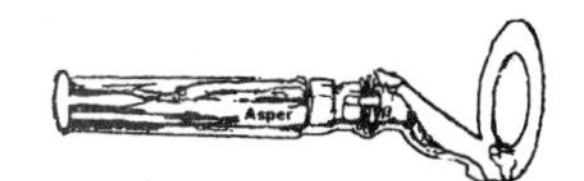

I understand what buzz is, but what is buzz pitch?

Buzz pitch is the actual pitch made by the buzz, or lip vibration, inside the mouthpiece cup/visualizer rim. This pitch controls the quality of the sound made on the trumpet. Phrases such as "that horn has a big sound" are misleading and generally not true. Horn design has some effect on the sound, but it is the trumpet player's technique that has more effect upon the breadth and depth of the sound they can produce. The smallest horn *can* produce a big open sound – just as a large horn *can* produce a narrow, pinched sound. It is true, however, that some horns are built so that the big open sound is easier to achieve. The key to remember is that *breadth and depth of the trumpet sound is directly related to the pitch of the buzz inside the mouthpiece cup – the lower the buzz pitch, the wider the sound.*

Can the buzz pitch be controlled?

The buzz pitch can be controlled two ways. The first is by contracting and relaxing the lips as they vibrate inside the mouthpiece cup/visualizer rim. The second is by moving both the teeth and the lips together – essentially a biting motion. I recommend that you use only the first method. In the second method, the biting action results in thinning out the tone, and it is much more difficult to control than the first method. Using the first method when practicing the mouthpiece/visualizer buzzing routine will allow you to control the width of the contractions and learn the point at which the width makes the pitch out of tune. This control will come with practice.

Is the buzz pitch something that can be practiced?

Yes. It is one reason why I wrote this book. I was never much of a 'practice the buzz' person until I realized how much effect it had on my playing. I am *still not* an advocate of practicing the buzz without the horn or mouthpiece/visualizer up on the embouchure due to the fact that there is a risk of closing the throat. However, daily *mouthpiece* buzzing will give you control over buzz pitch by isolating the reflex groups that control the contraction/relaxation of the lips. A more relaxed buzz will result.

What will the relaxed buzz achieve?

The relaxed buzz will translate into a fairly low buzz pitch and a wider, warmer sound. The exercises, all done with access to a piano, (see Appendices), will start on a fairly low-pitched piano note for each of the three mouthpieces (alto horn, Asper Visualizer, and trumpet mouthpiece).

Figure 13 Starting piano pitches

As we progress through the exercises, certain changes will be expected. As we ascend from the lowest pitch for each mouthpiece/visualizer, we will expect to see and to feel more firmness in the embouchure.

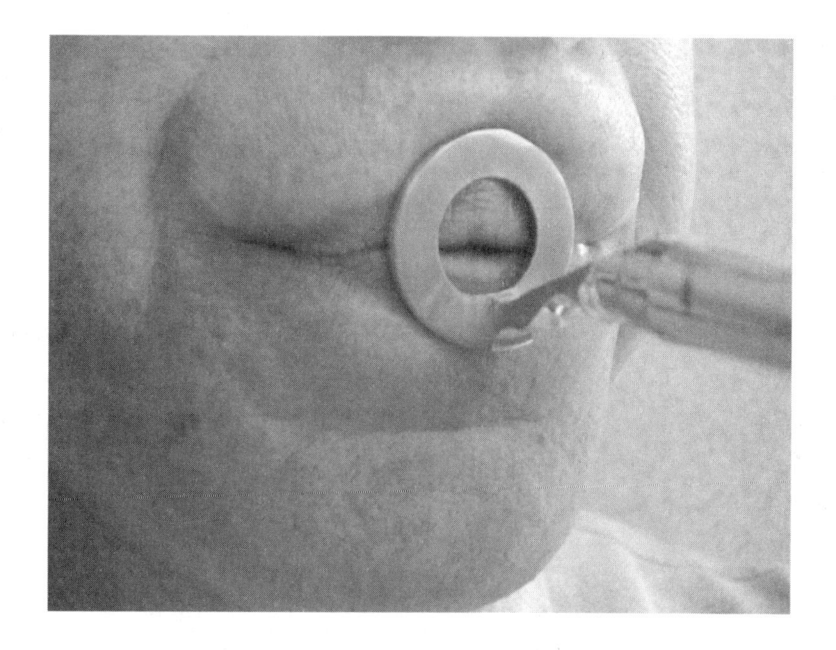

Figure 14 Relaxed embouchure

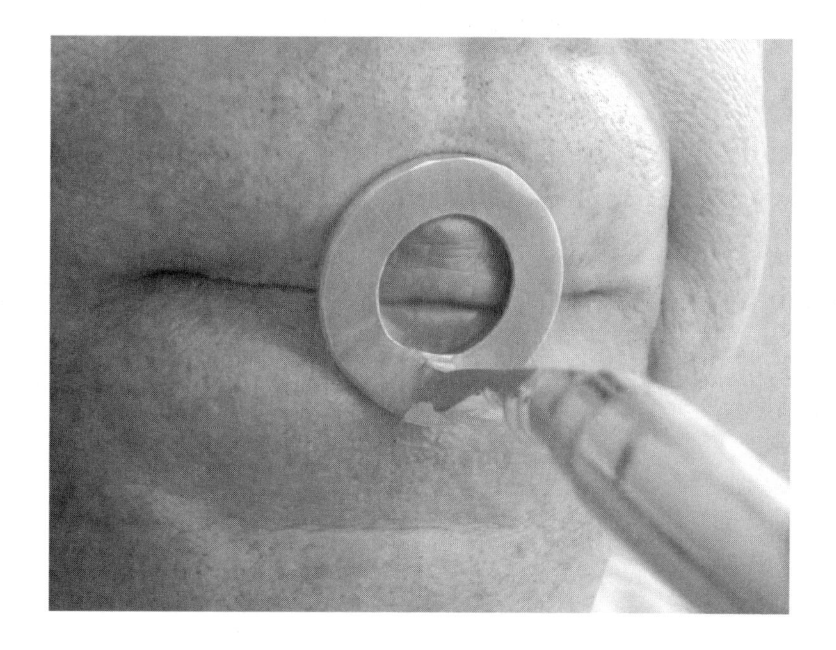

Figure 15 Firm embouchure

Unit 7 Buzzing

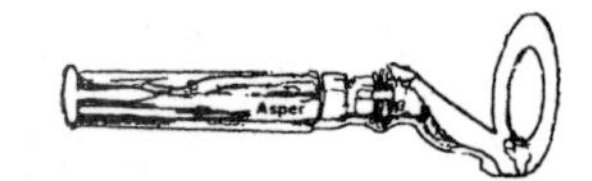

What do I need to understand about buzzing?

The embouchure is where the buzz occurs and is the focal point of not only this book, but brass playing in general. I know that terminology can get confusing, and that many teachers use the same terms in slightly different ways. I'll try to be very clear about the way I use terms and why.

I will describe the opening between the lips as the **aperture**. As stated before, the lips are independent vibrators and only begin vibrating when air is blown between them at a specific velocity. At this specific velocity they will begin to vibrate.

The photograph below shows the **aperture**. The lips are rolled in slightly and the embouchure muscles are somewhat firm. Yet notice how wide open it measures vertically and horizontally. It is wider than the outside diameter of an average trumpet mouthpiece rim (1.070 inches).

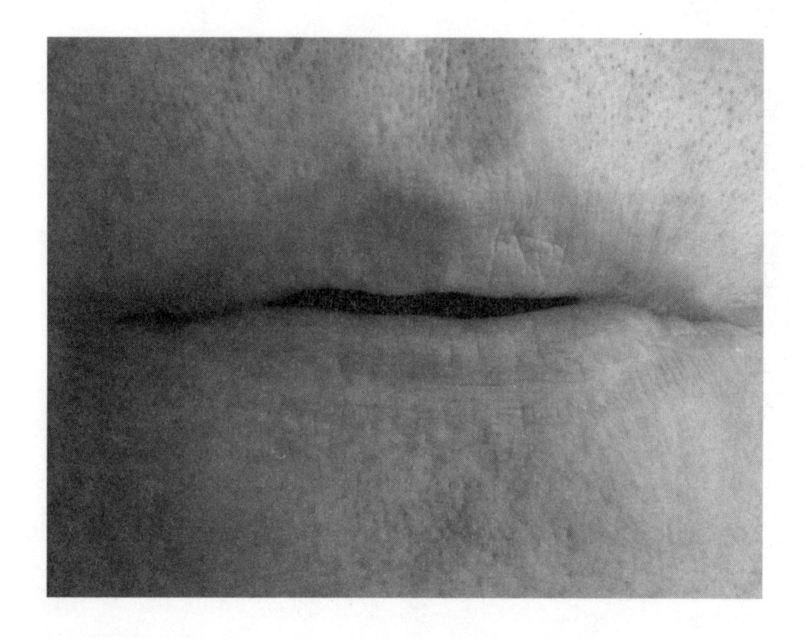

Figure 16

The aperture

This photograph is the identical photograph with vertical lines drawn to indicate where the edges of a tuba mouthpiece might rest.

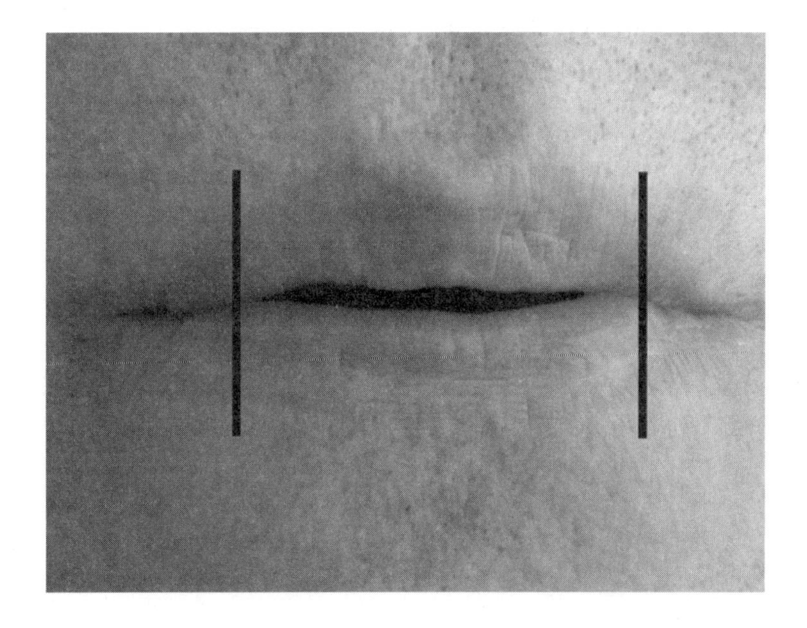

Figure 17 Edges of a tuba mouthpiece

This photograph represents a trombone mouthpiece.

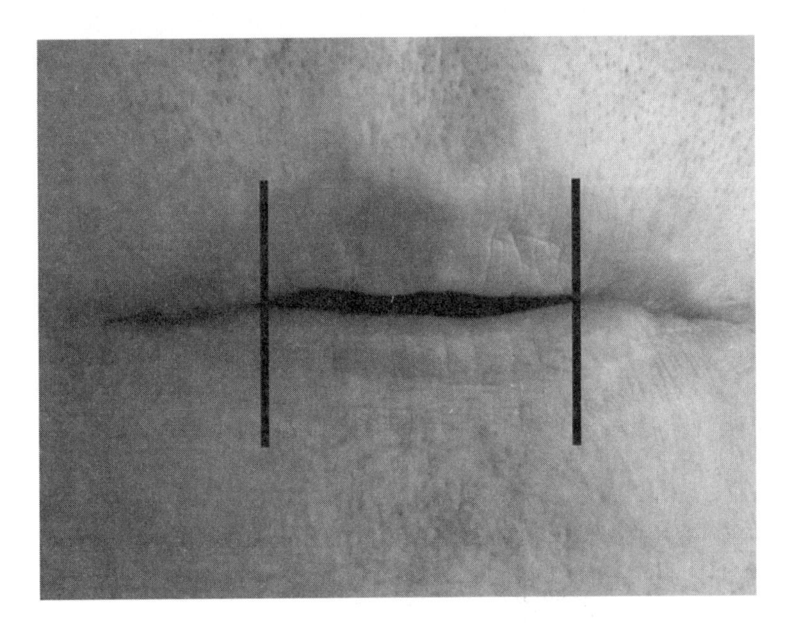

Figure 18 Edges of a trombone mouthpiece

Finally we have the trumpet mouthpiece rim width.

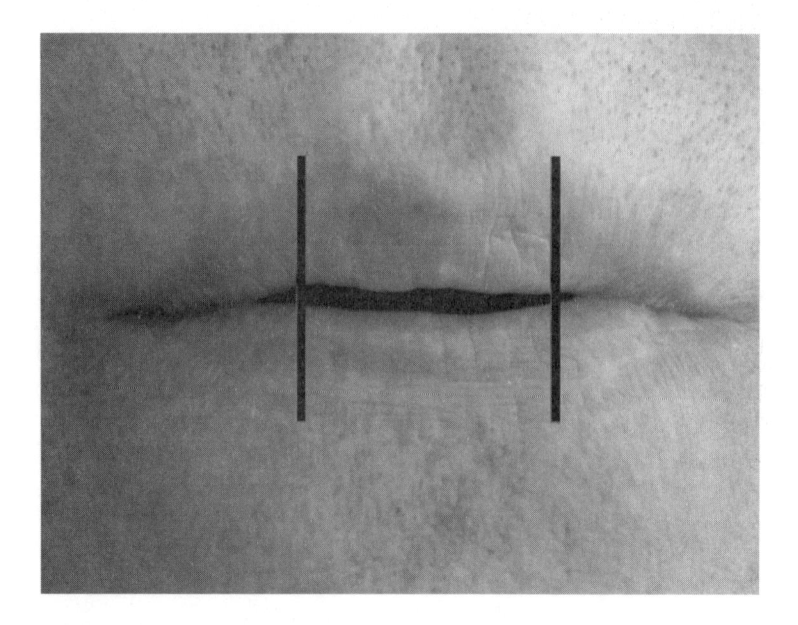

Figure 19 Edges of a trumpet mouthpiece

I am attempting to show that each time we place a smaller rim size on the aperture, the lips will vibrate at a pitch depending upon a combination of how much room they have horizontally (width of aperture), and how much space there is in which to vibrate (the total size of the inside of the cup).

We get the same result in buzz pitch when moving between trumpet rim sizes and cup depths. As the rim gets smaller and the cup gets shallower, the buzz pitch gets higher.

Can this be demonstrated somehow?

Yes. As I said before, I am not an advocate of buzzing without any mouthpiece, but let's try this experiment *just once*.

Go to a mirror and try to form the aperture the way I show in the next photograph. Notice the lips are rolled in slightly and that the facial muscles are fairly firm. If your lips are fleshy you will not need to roll in as much.

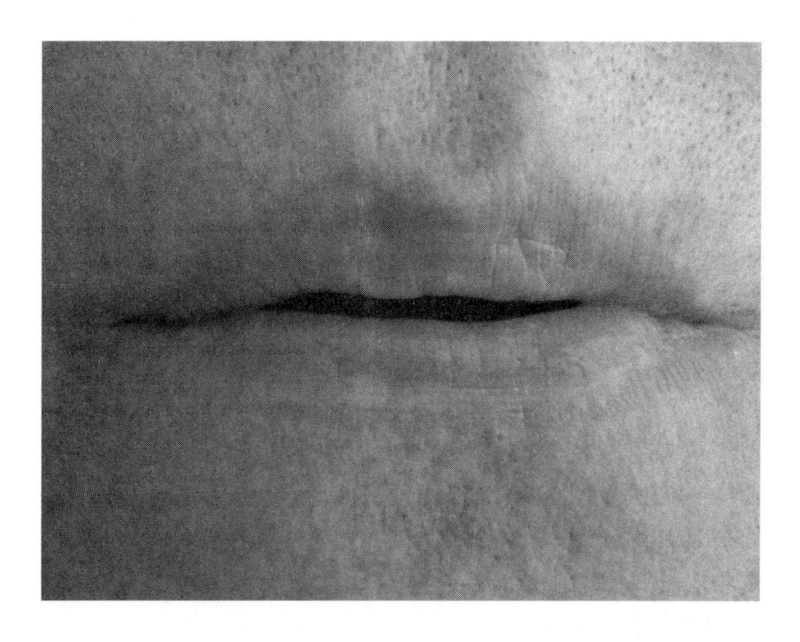

Figure 20 The aperture

Place your index fingers in front of your lips without touching them. Now blow air through the aperture, but don't blow hard enough to get the buzz started. *Just blow air.* While the air stream is being blown between the lips, gently touch your index fingers vertically to your lips in much the same position as in Figure 17 with the tuba mouthpiece vertical lines.

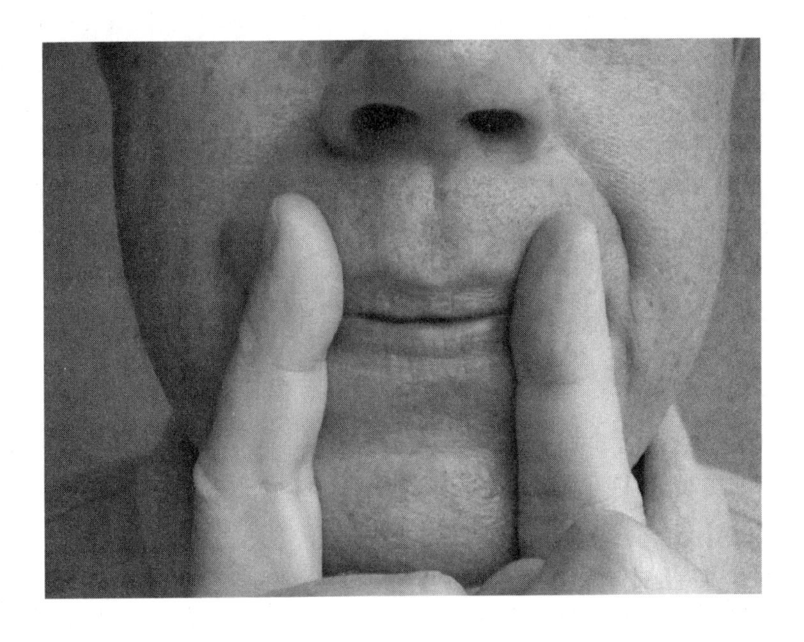

Figure 21 Tuba fingers with the buzz

Did you notice that it takes *very little pressure from your fingers* to get the buzz to start?

Now, try repeating this with the other photographs as guides.

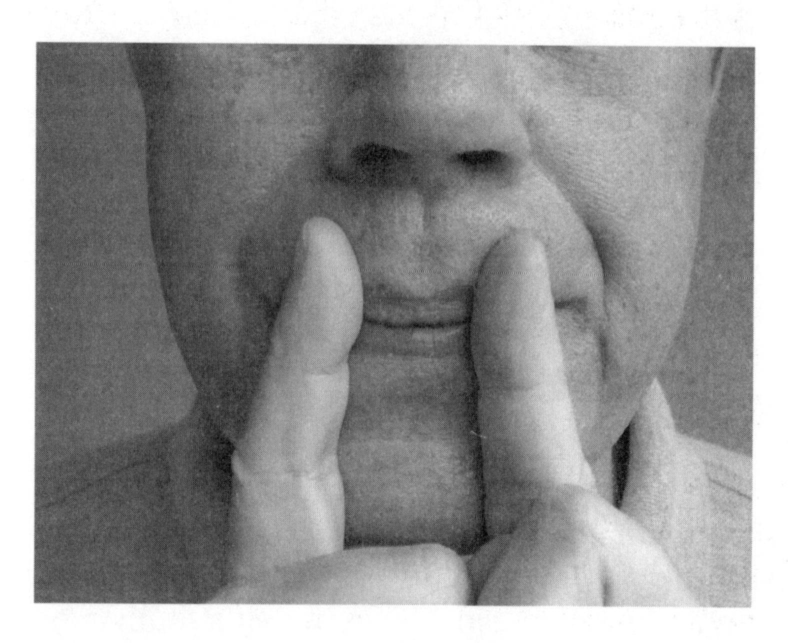

Figure 22 Trombone fingers with the buzz

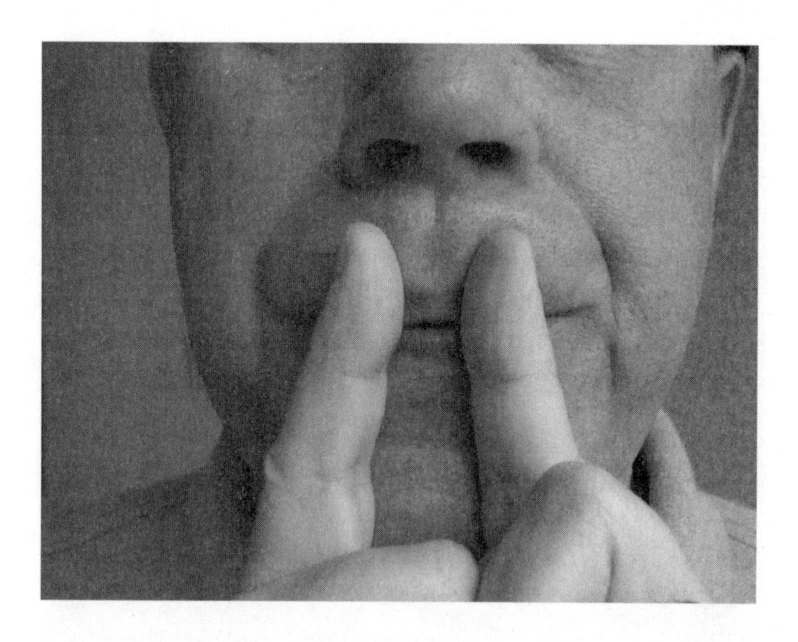

Figure 23 Trumpet fingers with the buzz

This exercise demonstrates that it is the placement of the sides of the mouthpiece rim that controls the relative buzz pitch. The rim cuts off the width of the vibration. It also demonstrates that *very little mouthpiece weight is needed to get the buzz started!*

Then what is the job of the top and the bottom of the mouthpiece rim?

This is where the actual mouthpiece rim size becomes important. Remember what I discussed in Unit 4 on embouchure? *Play on muscle!*

We need to play on a trumpet mouthpiece rim size that is large enough so that the top and the bottom of the mouthpiece are placed on muscle (orbicularis oris). If the mouthpiece rim size is too small, the top and bottom will only sit on flesh. Flesh alone has very little strength and the player will tire easily. If a mouthpiece rim size is too large, a tremendous amount of embouchure strength is required to play for a long time. The same is true for playing in the upper register. This translates into many more hours of practice each day (to develop that embouchure strength) in order to achieve the same results as a player who is using the correct rim size.

Unit 8 Lip Shape

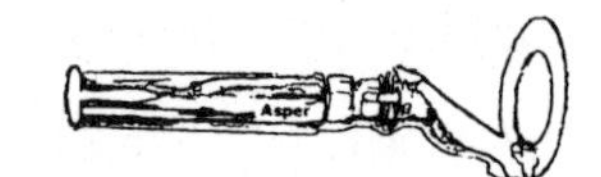

How can I tell if I'm playing on the correct rim size?

For ease of discussion I will use the Bach rim sizes as a standard for comparison throughout this book.

It seems as though a tradition was established many years ago of placing a 7C mouthpiece in every 'starter' or student model trumpet case. My experience has shown that many trumpet mouthpiece difficulties begin at that point – even if the 7C rim size is appropriate. This is even more troublesome as the young trumpet player matures and does not change mouthpieces at the appropriate time in the physical maturation process. Many young people have facial structures that would demand a larger rim size, especially as they grow older.

In order to select the correct size mouthpiece, you must have a sense of how much flesh you will be putting in that mouthpiece to vibrate. You need to become aware of your lips and unique facial structure.

How do I know what facial structure I have?

Compare your own facial structure to the following examples:

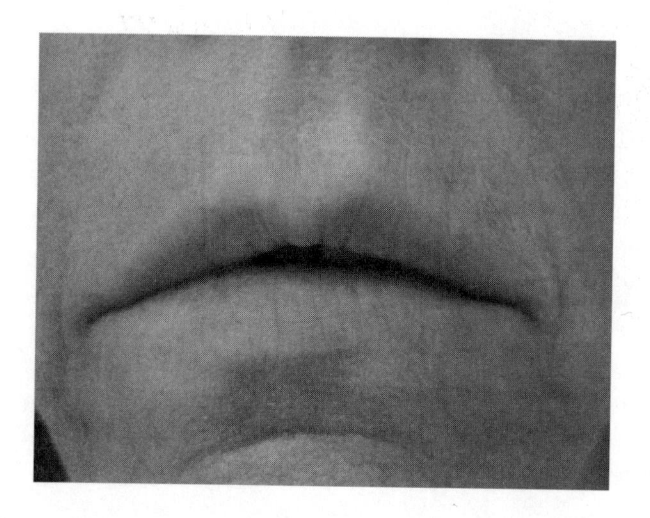

Figure 24

Thin lips – adult female

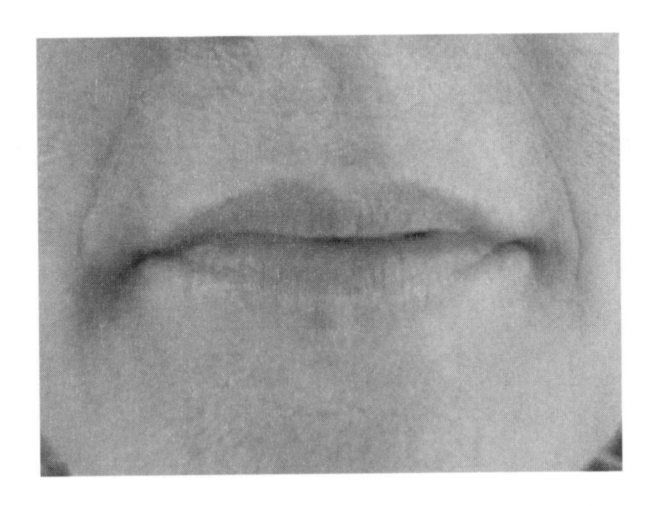

Figure 25

Average lips - adult female

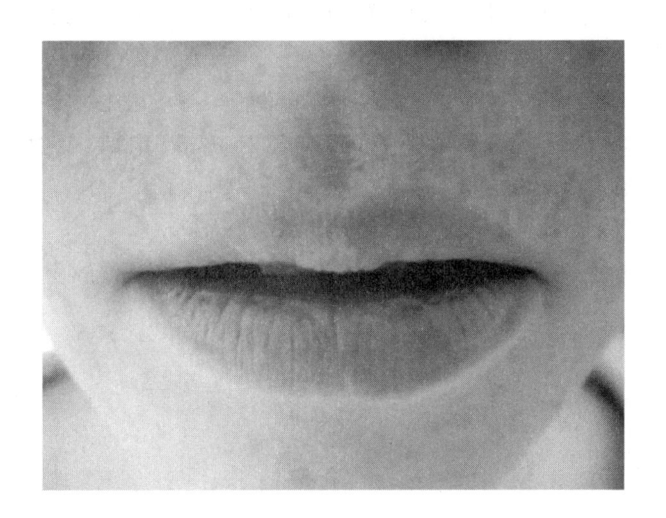

Figure 26

Average lips with semi-teardrop shaped upper lip – adult female

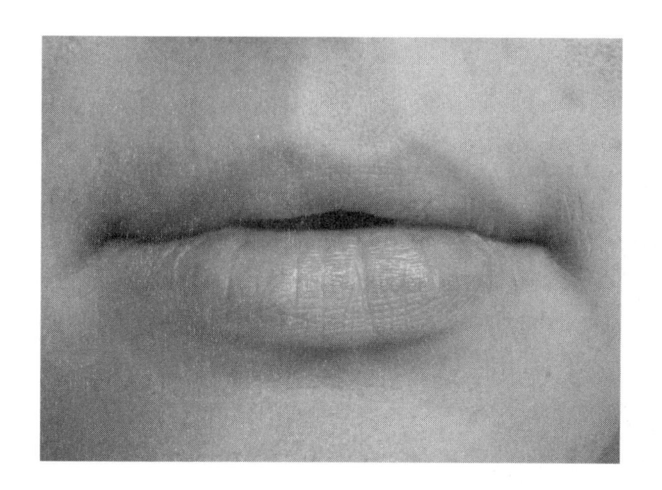

Figure 27

Fleshy lips – Adult female

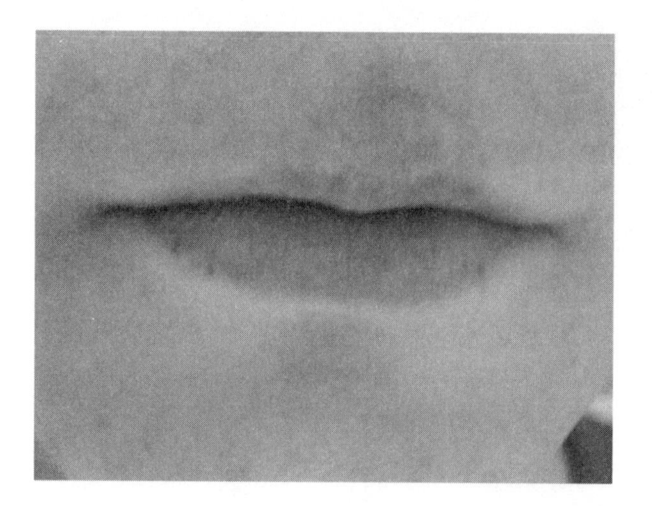

Figure 28

Thin lips – adult male

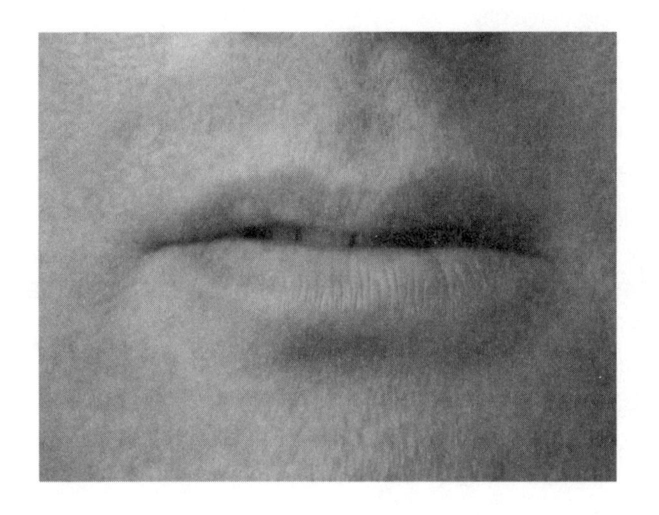

Figure 29

Average lips – adult male

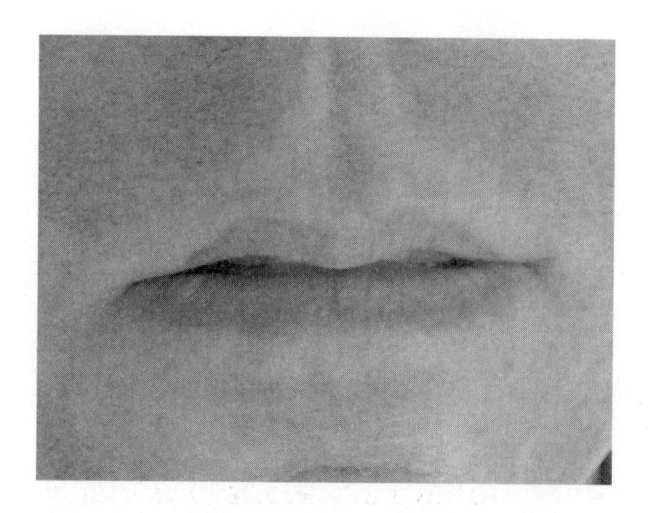

Figure 30

Average lips with a semi-teardrop shaped upper lip – adult male

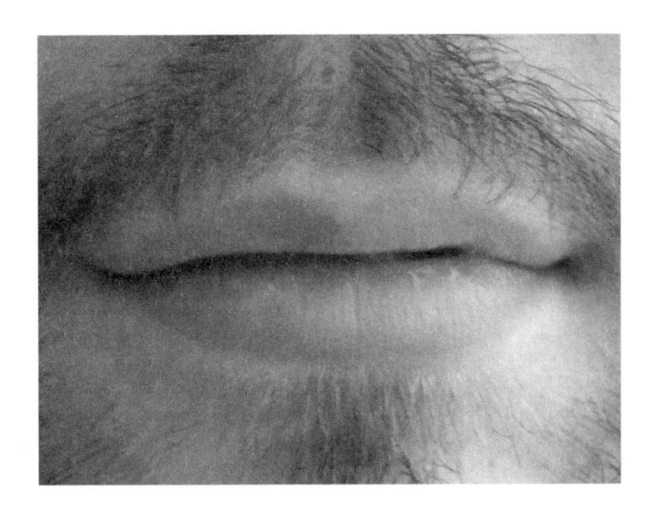

Figure 31

Fleshy lips – adult male

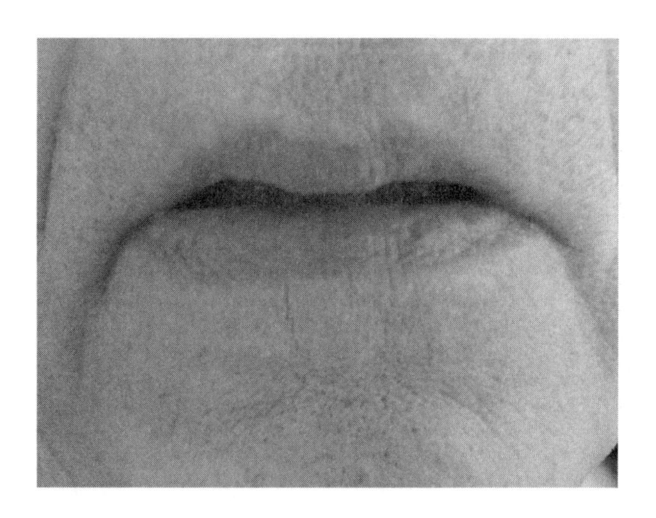

Figure 32

Fleshy lips with a teardrop shaped upper lip – adult male

As we progress from thin to average to fleshy, then semi-teardrop to teardrop, you can imagine all of the variations in between. Without making this too complicated, we must remember that *the lips must have enough room to vibrate efficiently inside the cup of the mouthpiece!*

How can I see this for myself?

You can see this by using a ***trumpet mouthpiece visualizer*** *that is the same rim size as the mouthpiece you play on the trumpet.*

I then use the mouthpiece visualizer in two different ways. **The rim size is of utmost importance.**

Initially I use the trumpet mouthpiece visualizer as a diagnostic tool. I want to be able to see the buzz inside the rim vibrating exactly as it does inside the real trumpet mouthpiece.

What should I be looking or listening for?

These four things:

1. *Aperture width*
   - *The width of the aperture should extend across the entire diameter of the inside of the rim while buzzing*
2. *Amount of upper lip inside the rim*
   - *The upper lip should account for 50-55% of the vibrating surface inside the rim. 55-60% would be best*
3. *The width of the sound of the buzz*
   - *The buzz should be loud. Use lots of air*
4. *The ability to buzz through a pre-described buzz range*
   - *The player should be able to start on middle C on the piano continuing down to C below middle C*
   - *The player should be able to start on middle C on the piano continuing up to F on the top of the treble clef staff*

You said you use the visualizer in two different ways. What is the second?

After using the visualizer as a diagnostic tool, I then use it each day to check the reflex groups that pertain to the buzz, pivot and embouchure. Then I use the visualizer to maintain (practice) correct reflexes each day.

In A Physical Approach to Playing the Trumpet, I talk extensively about building the body's reflexes in order to play the trumpet efficiently. I will not go into as much detail in this book, but I need to say just a few things about reflex building.

Unit 9 Reflexes

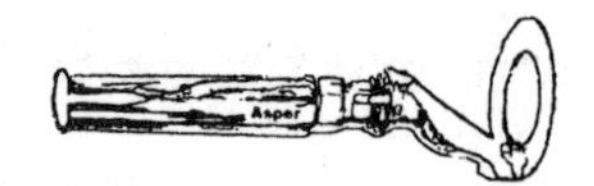

What are reflexes, and how are they used in trumpet playing?

> **reflex** \'re-fleks\ n. 1. An automatic and often inborn response to a stimulus that involves a nerve impulse passing inward from a receptor to a nerve center and thence outward to an effector (muscle or gland) without reaching the level of consciousness

One way to interpret this definition is to see reflexes as only those inborn physical actions over which we have no control. An example of this type of interpretation would be the pupils of your eyes dilating when the lights dim or your leg moving when the doctor taps your knee with a small mallet. In a broader sense, we can think of reflexes as physical actions learned over time and by repetition that become so automatic that you no longer have to think about them to make them happen – any more than you think about your pupils! What if those automatic reflexes could be applied to trumpet playing?

When we were small children, at some time we learned about *hot.* Our parents said, "Don't you touch that, it's hot!" Well, we touched it anyway, and it *was* hot, and we got burned. The next time our parents said, "Don't touch that, it's hot!" we thought about it for a minute, we *still* touched it, and we got burned again. After several encounters with outdoor grills, electric heaters, stoves etc., we not only learned to listen to our parents, but our bodies learned something as well. Our sense of touch identified extreme heat in a split second and sent a signal to the brain to pull the hand away from the heat. This learned and now automatic response is called a *reflex.* We no longer go through the thought processes to react to extreme heat – our body has learned to automatically respond correctly. Reflexes like the one in this example save us from harm, save us time, and free up the conscious part of the brain to concentrate on other activities.

How are these reflexes built and maintained?

Our bodies build and maintain hundreds and hundreds of different reflexes through repetition. For many of the musical reflexes, we initially have to use conscious thought to know how to respond. After the reflex is developed, our conscious thoughts are available to deal with other activities such as sight-reading, counting, or following the conductor. In order for the musician to develop all of the necessary reflexes required to be successful, repetition must be specific and frequent – it's called *practice.*

Is repetition of a reflex always a good thing?

Players sometimes feel as if their playing skills have leveled off or reached a plateau. These are players who, through no fault of their own, have developed bad physical playing habits – reflexes, which they unknowingly reinforce every day by their constant use. In this case, repetition of a reflex *can* be a bad thing. If the reflex you learned wasn't good to begin with, practicing it won't make it better!

How are reflexes triggered?

One way to trigger a reflex is by conscious thought. I have players use this method in the beginning when learning each reflex group. Once the proper reflex is practiced by repetition, less and less conscious thought is required.

Most of the time reflexes are triggered by our senses. When playing the trumpet, the ones we use mostly are sight, hearing, and, to a certain extent, touch.

Do reflexes ever decay?

Absolutely! If reflexes are not continually and properly reinforced, they *will* decay. If they are reinforced improperly, they will develop improperly. We will refer to correct practice as *conscious thought reflex building* or *conscious thought practice.* We will use conscious thought reflex building as part of the warm-up every day.

How many trumpet playing reflexes are there?

I have identified eight trumpet playing reflex groups. Some have already been discussed in earlier units. They are listed separately here for convenience and ease of learning. Actually, all eight are inter-related and learning one reflex group often depends upon learning other reflex groups. Development and application of each reflex group listed is described in detail in A Physical Approach to Playing the Trumpet.

1. Body Carriage (position of the head, arms/shoulders, legs/feet, and hands)
2. Embouchure (position of the muscles of the mouth and face)
3. Air Intake (the breathing mechanism)
4. Tongue Strike (how the buzz gets started)
5. Tongue Height (controls the speed of the air through the mouth)
6. Anchor (location of the weight of the mouthpiece/visualizer/trumpet)
7. Pivot (movement of the anchor)
8. Air Column (the air blowing mechanism)

So, what do I need to do?

We need to make sure that your practice routine has structure and goals and continually works to help the mind learn to react correctly to incoming sensory information. Then the mind must respond by sending correct signals to the body for appropriate muscle responses. The muscles must be well developed and strong enough to be able to respond to the incoming signals.

I can see that embouchure, air intake, anchor, pivot and air column are all important things to work on each day, but what does this have to do with practicing on the visualizer every day?

I talked above about reflexes decaying. This decay happens very quickly in some cases, and will surely happen over time if the proper reflexes are not reinforced daily. It is also important that our reflexes are reinforced *correctly* as well as frequently. We don't want to unknowingly strengthen a reflex that is not correct in the first place.

Therefore, I want to check the buzz with the visualizer *every day!* Again, this reflex reinforcement is done during the warm-up period each day.

I've been practicing this some and have realized that the buzz does not want to start right away. Is there something happening with my tonguing or is it something else?

If the buzz does not want to start right away it could be due to several factors that may include tonguing. I'll talk about tonguing next, and discuss the other factors when I talk about each mouthpiece separately.

Unit 10 Tonguing

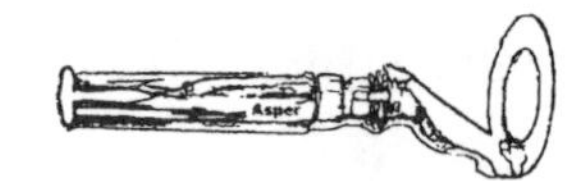

What tonguing technique should I use?

In talking to friends and reading trumpet technique books, I have found that I teach tonguing differently than most trumpet teachers. In the Preface I referred to the impact that my first trumpet teacher, Bob Ralston, had on my playing. Bob is a fine french horn player and he taught this tonguing technique to me. I suspect that the differences in how I teach tonguing may have to do with this exposure to french horn technique. I have met french horn players who tongue this way. However, I have not found many trumpet players who tongue the way I do. Generally speaking, the goal of tonguing is to produce sound with a clean, clear attack with no fuzzy or airy sound prior to the pitch. This must be possible at all tonguing speeds and dynamic levels. Here is how I approach tonguing.

In order for trumpet tone to be produced, the lips inside the cup of the mouthpiece need to buzz. We can get the lips to start buzzing by simply blowing air into the mouthpiece until the air speed is sufficient to start the lips buzzing, thus producing a sound. The sound, however, will be delayed because it takes some time for the air speed to get to a sufficient velocity to start the buzz. We need a little puff of air to help us create that air speed *immediately*. This is why we tongue.

Be wary of a tonguing technique which calls for the tongue to do 'its job' by touching the back of the upper teeth where the roof of the mouth meets the back of the upper front teeth, as if you were saying the word 'to' or 'tea'. The puff of air created by this technique then needs to drop down approximately ¼" in order to go between the teeth and get the buzz started. When I hear a player with a fuzzy and airy sound on the beginning of a note, I know what I'm hearing *is the actual sound of that puff of air dropping down and moving between the teeth.* One way to eliminate this airy attack is to tongue harder, creating a heavier puff. This is not a pleasant sound and it is not a technique I recommend.

What if you could create that puff of air closer to the lips? That would eliminate the need for the puff of air to have to travel to the lips to initiate the buzz, and it does not require the player to use a heavier tongue. To achieve this, the tongue could come between the teeth and actually touch the top lip right below the top teeth. This tongue placement is part of the tongue strike reflex group. The top lip is curled in slightly and pulled in against the top teeth making this technique very easy to use. Instead of the hard 'to' and 'tea' sounds, you should use the softer sounds; 'tho', 'thah', 'theh', 'thih' and 'thee'. This softer beginning sound places your tongue closer to your lips. The vowel sounds that follow the initial sound relate to air speed and pitch. One caution: *do not put the tongue between the teeth too early or too far out into the mouthpiece.* This causes a heavy, thudding sound I call 'pulling the plug'. Timing is everything!

This tongue strike tonguing technique allows you to tongue cleanly and eliminates the airy front on the note. It can be done with tremendous single tongue speed and can easily be applied to multiple tonguing after the single tonguing technique is learned. This technique also facilitates both staccato and legato tonguing styles because it allows for the buzz to be interrupted at precisely the point you desire. The buzz will then restart as the tongue is pulled away. This air stream interruption is the final step in the tongue strike reflex. Note that the word *strike* is not used in the context of harshness or hitting, but as in a 'snake' strike. The recoiling of the tongue is immediate and efficient, like the strike of a snake.

Let's make a list of all of the musical instruments we can think of which *do not require the vibrating material to be struck in some way.* (For this list we'll count plucking as striking.)

- Voice
- Flute
- Pipe organ
- Bagpipes
- Kazoo
- Harmonica

Why should playing a brass instrument be any different? I believe that touching the top lip (the most efficient vibrator) with your tongue is much more efficient than the alternative tongue strike at the back of the front teeth. I also have a suspicion that many trumpet players who believe that they are tonguing using the 'toe' or 'tee' method are not really using that approach at all.

What makes you say that?

When I first start using a mouthpiece visualizer with a player I never ask them how they are tonguing. Frankly, I don't want to know yet. I know that when I can 'see' the lips buzz in the visualizer I'll be able to tell which tonguing technique they are using to get the buzz started. I may even say nothing at that time. I'll wait until we move to the trumpet mouthpiece before I ask the 'tonguing' question. Many players say they are tonguing one way when in reality they are not. When I point out the discrepancy many players are amazed. It's mostly due to the fact that many trumpet players have never seen the buzz actually work inside the mouthpiece ring. They can't, because the cup is always in the way! *Visualizer practice will actually show you how you are tonguing and will help you decide which tonguing technique works best for you!* Once you have decided on a specific technique, daily visualizer practice will help you maintain and refine that technique.

How do these two tonguing techniques apply to the visualizer during the mouthpiece routine?

Through use of the visualizer you will discover whether or not the buzz is starting in an efficient manner because you can see the process as it occurs. Many players just get air with no buzz. Most of the time this is due to the fact that the aperture is too small (vertically and/or horizontally). Sometimes too much mouthpiece/visualizer pressure will cause the buzz not to start.

On the following page is a photograph of a normal relaxed buzz in the visualizer with an open aperture and lips not biting down on each other.

<u>This is what I look for in the mirror every morning!</u>

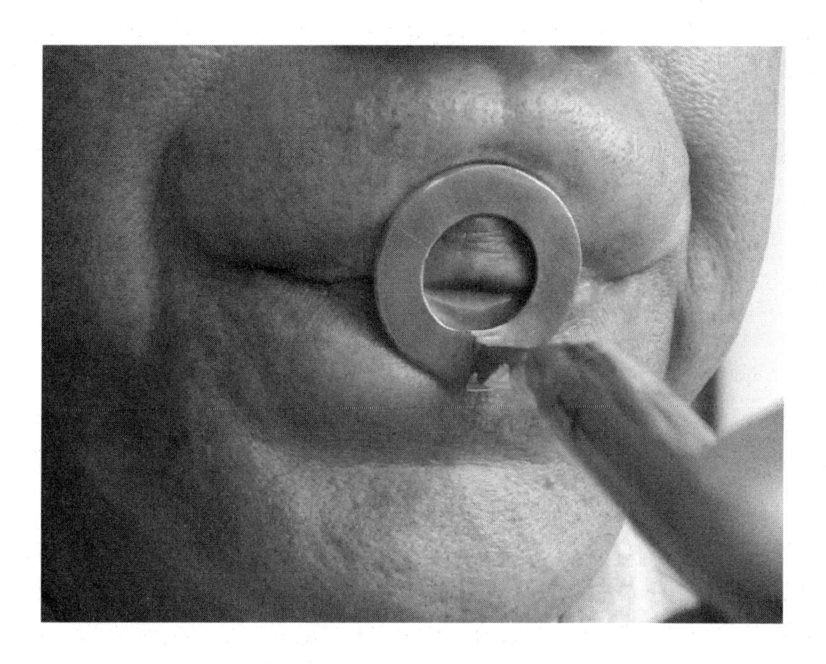

Figure 33 Normal buzz in the visualizer

Below is a photograph of me holding the aperture closed too tightly. I assure you that I'm getting nothing but air. If this were a video, you could see that the lips are not vibrating.

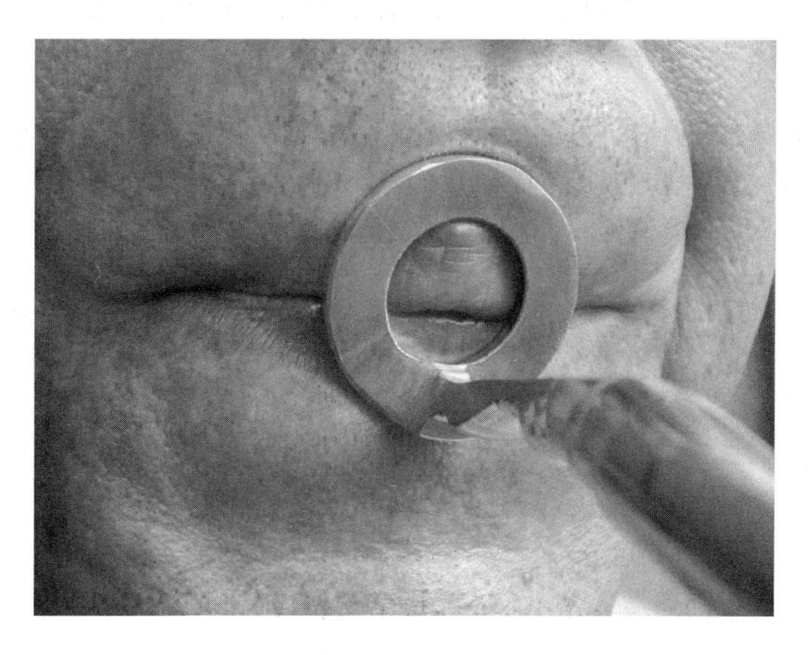

Figure 34 Pinched buzz with aperture closed

Now, using your visualizer or mouthpiece, apply the tonguing technique that you currently use. Does the buzz start cleanly or is there a delay in the vibration? If the buzz started cleanly with no 'air before the tone', then you are tonguing correctly for you. If the attack was not clean with the vibration beginning immediately, try the other tonguing technique. Remember, it's what works for *you*.

Unit 11 Daily Routine

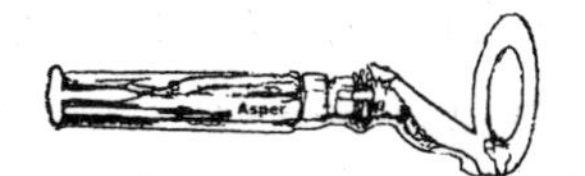

In what order do I use the mouthpieces during the mouthpiece routine?

Use the mouthpieces in this order:

1. Alto horn
2. Asper visualizer
3. Your mouthpiece
   (Remember, the visualizer and your mouthpiece must have the same rim size!)

What do I do with the alto horn mouthpiece?

We'll begin with the alto horn mouthpiece and use it in a variety of ways.

Remember what I stated in the introduction? The way we warm-up each day is controlled by what we did to ourselves the day before. If we had a normal playing day yesterday, then the work on the alto horn mouthpiece should take 5-7 minutes playing the exercises that are outlined in Appendix I.

There are four underlying goals for using the alto horn mouthpiece:

1. Take in plenty of air and blow it all out
2. Achieve a nice relaxed forte buzz
3. Develop a 'trumpet like' symmetry in the shape of the embouchure
4. Engage the brain and make a connection to the body

Stand in front of a mirror! Hold the alto horn mouthpiece as shown in the photograph below with the thumb and index finger of the left hand. Keep the other fingers relaxed.

Figure 35 Holding the alto horn mouthpiece

Holding the alto horn mouthpiece in this manner will prevent you from placing too much weight (pressure) on the embouchure. If you start to push up with your left hand, your thumb and index finger will start to slide up the shank of the alto horn mouthpiece. If this happens, you know you're playing with too much pressure on your embouchure.

Place the alto horn mouthpiece in the middle of your embouchure, take a deep breath and try to buzz a note somewhere between middle C on the piano and the G below middle C.

Figure 36 Initial alto horn buzz range

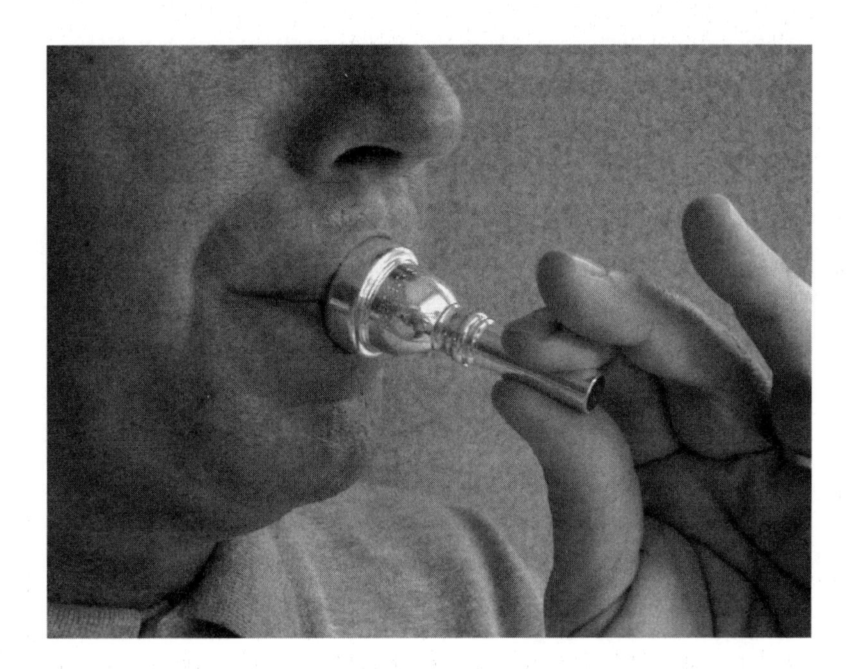

Figure 37 Alto horn mouthpiece on the embouchure

If you're successful the very first time, then you have established the proper starting range for the alto horn mouthpiece. If not, keep trying until you achieve a pitch within the initial buzz pitch range. If, when you try for the initial pitch, the note that results is way too high, you may be buzzing with an aperture that is too closed *or,* you may be pinching your lips together (biting). Remember, you must play forte. Blow the air!

You said to begin the alto horn section of the mouthpiece buzzing routine this way after a normal playing day. How should I change this if I had a very heavy playing day and/or abused my embouchure in some way?

This is quite common. I notice this mostly on the day after a brass quintet concert, a big 'show' of some kind, or a three or four set big band gig.

I spend quite a long time on the alto horn mouthpiece on these days. Some mornings my chops actually feel puffy. I may spend 15-25 minutes on the alto horn mouthpiece until my embouchure feels like I can go to the visualizer. I have, on occasion, spent more than 25 minutes on the alto horn mouthpiece. (This includes a lot of rest in between each exercise.)

We must remember that after a long or abusive day of playing, that puffy feeling the next morning is due to swelling of the lips. The lips have experienced 'tissue trauma' and are indeed swollen. It has been my experience that buzzing on the alto horn mouthpiece for a longer period of time the next morning helps my lips recover more quickly.

You talked earlier about the weight distribution (anchor and pivot) on your embouchure. Is this also important when using the alto horn mouthpiece?

I find that anchor and pivot are much less important when using this bigger mouthpiece. Remember, what is most important here is not how high or how low we're going to buzz on the alto horn mouthpiece. We must buzz in a very relaxed manner, taking in lots of air and blowing it all out with a consistent air stream, while maintaining a 'trumpet like' embouchure symmetry.

Does the angle at which the alto horn mouthpiece comes away from my face have any bearing yet?

Not really. We still want to see a fairly normal mouthpiece angle with this mouthpiece (see Figure 37). The angle issue will become much more critical when we move to the visualizer.

What kind of sound should I be listening for?

Work toward a sound that is big, wide, and loud. This type of sound will be the product of firmly engaging the internal and external oblique muscles of the abdomen while you consistently move the air stream.

You talked about tongue height before and how it affects the speed of the air as it passes through the mouth. Is this a factor with the alto horn mouthpiece buzz?

Tongue height is not too important yet, except when moving towards the upper register. The tongue height (air speed) issue will become more important when you start buzzing on the visualizer.

You stated that the range of buzz pitches is not as important on the alto horn mouthpiece. In what range will I be buzzing?

The exercises will start fairly low – between a middle C and a G below middle C on the piano (See page 22). The exercises will then progress up to C in the third space of the treble clef and down to F one space below the bass clef.

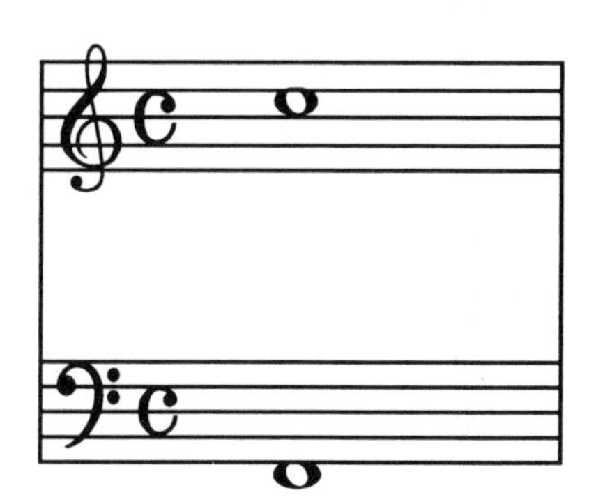

Figure 38 Alto horn buzz range

You talked about how to use the alto horn mouthpiece buzz after normal playing days and on days after some abuse occurred. Are there any other factors that could control how much time I spend on the alto horn mouthpiece?

Yes. Once or twice a year I do take a vacation from trumpet playing. When I come back to the instrument from time off, I start with long periods of time buzzing on the alto horn mouthpiece in front of the mirror (15-20 minutes three times a day for a couple of days). This approach lets me get back to concentrating on the look and the feel of having a mouthpiece on my face again. I know I'm not going to rush for results. I know it's going to take time to get back to where I was. I concentrate instead on the feeling of the mouthpiece on my embouchure, the feeling of the breathing apparatus as I blow the air stream, and the very relaxed feeling of the buzz as the air stream moves through the mouthpiece.

How will I know when it's time to move to the visualizer?

Try as best you can to play the exercises outlined in Appendix I for 5-7 minutes on the alto horn mouthpiece (normal day). Make a note of the upper and lower extremes that you were able to achieve on the exercise and then move on to the visualizer. Try to extend your range, playing higher and lower each day until you can play the entire exercise.

Eventually, you will write your own exercises. I will explain this process later in Appendix IV.

Unit 12 The Visualizer

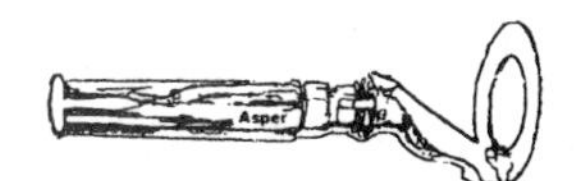

How can I start to think about using a visualizer if I don't know whether or not I'm playing on the correct sized mouthpiece?

It is through the use of the visualizer that you will be able to determine whether or not your mouthpiece is the correct size. If you know you have the trumpet that will do the job for you, but you can't seem to find the correct mouthpiece to get the sound you are trying to achieve, you may have to test several visualizers before you settle on one rim size. It would be best to find a teacher who has a basic visualizer set to help you through this part of mouthpiece fitting. (If a teacher is not available, write or call me!)

Wait a minute; you just introduced the trumpet as another variable. When should I consider the trumpet in mouthpiece/visualizer selection?

You may want to consider the trumpet first. Playing the trumpet is **always about the sound.** If you're a great technical player with a poor sound, no one will want to listen. If you are a player who does most playing in a bright idiom (jazz, pop, brass quintet) you will tend to pick an instrument that achieves that sound efficiently. If you tend to play in a darker/wider idiom (symphony orchestra, concert band, solo playing) you will tend to pick an instrument that will achieve that sound efficiently. If you do all kinds of playing, you will pick an instrument that achieves both sounds efficiently, then vary the mouthpiece cup depth or cup shape to achieve the sound you need at the moment. *The visualizer/mouthpiece rim size, however, will remain the same!*

If you do not like your present sound, ask yourself these questions. Is your trumpet built for the kind of playing mentioned in the paragraph above? If the answer is 'no', you should get an instrument that does. If the answer was 'yes', you should now fit the visualizer/mouthpiece to the instrument.

Does this mean that I may need to try several Asper Visualizers before I make up my mind which rim size fits my embouchure?

It is possible. The 'mystery' here is whether or not you're playing on the correct mouthpiece rim in the first place. However, some factors have an affect here. If you are in high school and are still playing on the rim you played on when you were a beginner, you probably need to try some other rims. If you are in college or are an older player and you're still using the rim size you used in high school, you probably need to reconsider the rim size. If you have gained or lost a considerable amount of weight, you may need to reconsider the size of the rim.

Why?

You've grown! If you can determine through your parents and family what percentage of your adult height and weight you have achieved, you can make a reasonably intelligent guess about how much more you will grow. Obviously much of our growth comes when we're younger. It then stands to reason that a rim that fits when we're in fifth or sixth grade will probably not work when we're in tenth or eleventh grade. Another change may occur during your collegiate years. Most of the time, when these factors are considered, players need more room for their lips to vibrate. This translates into the need for a larger rim size (interior diameter measurement), deeper cup depth, wider rim, or a combination of these.

How do I use the Asper Visualizer?

Let's refresh our memory using the photograph from Unit 7 that shows air being blown through the open aperture.

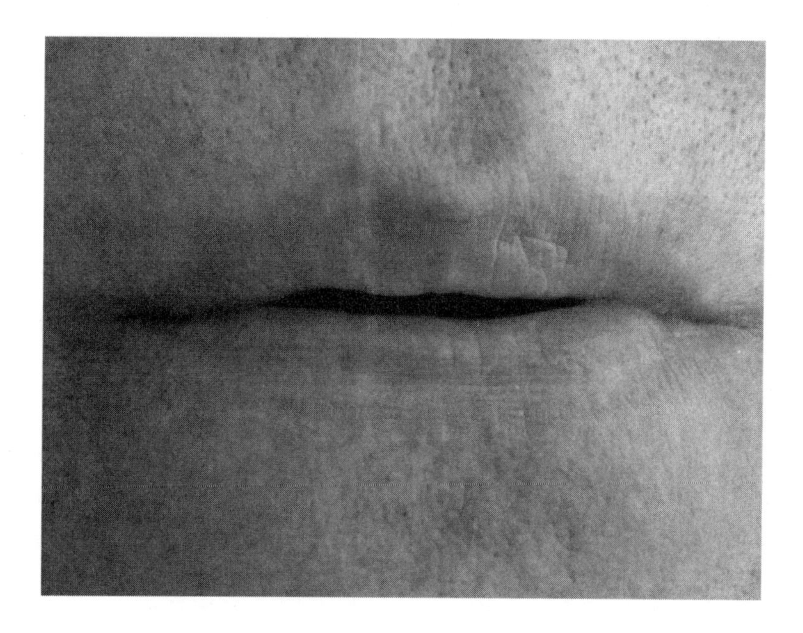

Figure 39 The aperture

Let's also recall our previous discussion about altering the aperture with our fingers so that it is the width of the trumpet mouthpiece.

Figure 40 Trumpet fingers with the buzz

Using the previous two photographs as a guide, look in the mirror and place the Asper Visualizer on the bottom lip. Place it on the bottom lip where you currently place your trumpet mouthpiece.

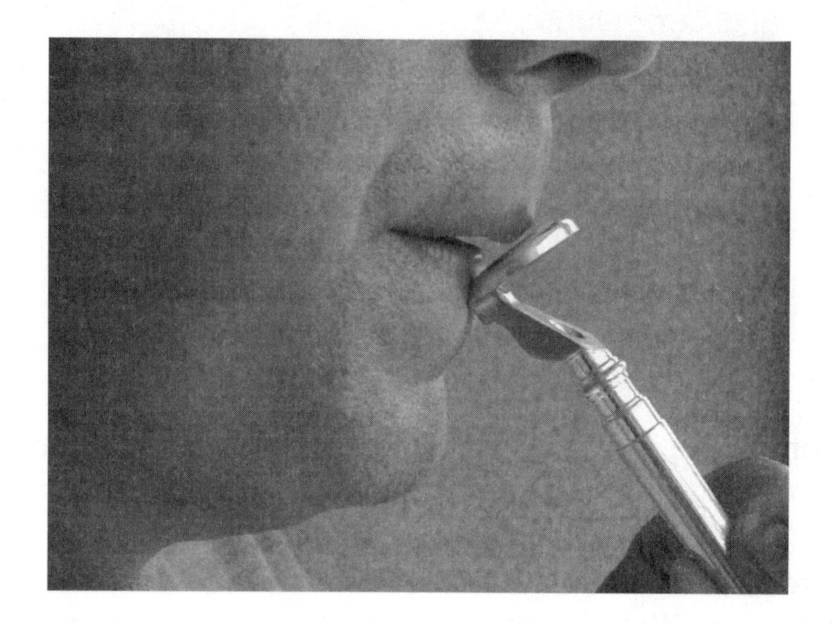

Figure 41 Visualizer placement on bottom lip

Take a deep 'ho' breath and start to blow the air stream gently through the aperture *without* sufficient air speed to get the buzz started. As you continue blowing, *slowly* tip the Asper Visualizer up onto your upper lip. Did the buzz start? If it did, did you notice how much pressure it took on the upper lip to get the buzz started? How open was the aperture when the buzz started?

In Unit 8, you may have been able to determine your physical type with or without the use of a mirror. Your initial experience with the Asper Visualizer will give you information about the inner diameter measurement of the visualizer that your facial structure will require. You may know right away if you are playing on a visualizer that has the correct or incorrect inside diameter.

How will I know?

You will know if the buzz starts right away with very little pressure on the embouchure. This is an indication that the inside diameter of the visualizer rim is correct for you.

If you know that you have fleshy lips you may need slightly more pressure on the lips in order to get them to vibrate. If your lips are not particularly fleshy, you may be able to use less pressure, roll your lips in slightly and use your muscular control to open and close the aperture inside the visualizer rim.

If, while placing the visualizer on your top lip, you noticed that you pull upper lip *out* of the rim, you *are playing on a rim that is too small.* What's happening is that your body knows that there is too much lip inside the rim of the visualizer to vibrate, so it has built a reflex to pull lip out each time you set the visualizer on your embouchure. This harmful 'pulling lip out' motion may place the top of the visualizer *under the orbicularis oris muscle* *(see page 14).* You are then placing the visualizer on flesh with no muscle under the rim. This will cause early fatigue and interfere with the amount of control you have over your sound.

If your buzz started right away without much pressure on the lips, you are probably pretty close to the correct rim size. If the buzz did not speak and you have fleshy lips, put a little more visualizer weight on the top lip. If you have fleshy lips and more pressure does not get the buzz started, you may need to try a larger rim size.

Is there a guide or chart that will help me make some decisions about mouthpiece rim sizes?

Yes. Gerald Endsley has written a book entitled <u>Comparative Mouthpiece Guide for Trumpet</u>. In this book Mr. Endsley has taken measurements of mouthpieces from some of the most popular mouthpiece manufacturers so that we can compare them by brand and rim size number, inside cup diameter, outside cup diameter, rim width and cup depth. (If you would like a copy of this book, see the bibliography section on page 88). If you're a teacher, you need this book!

Mr. Endsley has given me permission to duplicate pages from his book. As I mentioned earlier, I will refer exclusively to Bach sizes and measurements in this book. I have, therefore, provided you with the Bach information only.

How do I use this chart?

Look at the far left side of the chart and find the rim size on which you are currently playing. If, when starting the buzz, you felt that you needed a slightly smaller or larger rim size, move to the next logical size.

When you look at the chart remember that the most important information used in determining the correct rim size for the Asper Visualizer (or any mouthpiece) is the *inside diameter.* It is the inside diameter that determines how wide the aperture will be when the visualizer/mouthpiece is placed on the embouchure. If there was no buzz, or you needed too much pressure to get the buzz started, or you saw that you were pulling lip out of the mouthpiece rim, you may need to try a larger inside rim diameter. But look carefully at this chart. ***Many of the inside diameters are identical as you move up and down rim size numbers.*** *Many trumpet players do not know this!*

Endsley Chart

Bach Rim Size	Inside Diameter	Outside Diameter	Cup Depth	Rim Width
1	.671	1.078	.472	.407
1C	.671	1.076	.527	.405
1¼C	.671	1.080	.541	.409
1½C	.671	1.070	.538	.399
2	.655	1.056	.520	.401
2C	.655	1.056	.529	.401
2½C	.655	1.073	.446	.418
2¾	.655	1.058	.472	.403
3	.655	1.070	.533	.415

Bach Rim Size	Inside Diameter	Outside Diameter	Cup Depth	Rim Width
3C	.655	1.077	.495	.422
5A	.655	1.072	.591	.417
5B	.655	1.062	.531	.407
5C	.655	1.070	.509	.415
6	.655	1.067	.478	.412
6B	.655	1.071	.530	.416
6C	.655	1.066	.533	.411
7	.655	1.069	.498	.414
7A	.655	1.060	.587	.405
7BW	.655	1.106	.500	.451
7C	.655	1.060	.562	.405
7CW	.655	1.102	.533	.447
7D	.655	1.064	.490	.409
7E	.655	1.070	.487	.415
7EW	.655	1.094	.484	.439
8	.655	1.078	.492	.423
8B	.655	1.065	.495	.410
8C	.655	1.086	.482	.431
8½	.640	1.057	.535	.417
8½A	.640	1.066	.564	.426
8½B	.640	1.053	.496	.413
8½C	.640	1.058	.538	.418
8¾	.640	1.039	.549	.399
8¾C	.640	1.040	.510	.400
9	.640	1.053	.510	.413
9A	.640	1.044	.542	.404
9B	.640	1.055	.490	.415
9C	.640	1.053	.506	.413
9D	.640	1.057	.551	.417
10	.624	1.063	.539	.439
10B	.624	1.051	.508	.427
10C	.624	1.052	.483	.428
10½A	.624	1.040	.575	.416

Bach Rim Size	Inside Diameter	Outside Diameter	Cup Depth	Rim Width
10½C	.624	1.053	.533	.429
10½D	.624	1.062	.509	.438
10½DW	.624	1.075	.500	.451
10½E	.624	1.065	.502	.441
10½W	.624	1.175	.540	.551
10¾A	.624	1.041	.577	.417
10¾CW	.624	1.137	.419	.513
10¾EW	.624	1.131	.427	.507
11A	.624	1.053	.589	.429
11B	.624	1.041	.524	.417
11C	.624	1.066	.476	.442
11D	.624	1.067	.484	.443
11DW	.624	1.168	.458	.544
11EW	.624	1.170	.410	.546
11½C	.624	1.070	.534	.517
11½W	.624	1.022	.556	.398
11¾C	.608	1.065	.507	.457
11¾CW	.608	1.075	.507	.467
12	.608	1.049	.507	.441
12B	.608	1.042	.508	.434
12C	.608	1.045	.476	.437
12CW	.608	1.175	.516	.567
17	.593	1.033	.537	.440
17C	.593	1.042	.450	.449
18	.593	1.077	.504	.484
18C	.593	1.084	.502	.491
20C	.593	1.051	.523	.458

Let's start in the middle of the Bach rim size column. You'll notice that the inside diameter of the mouthpiece rims between the 8C and the 2 are the same. The inside diameter *does not change* as we move from a 7C to a 5C to a 3C*!* What *does* change as we move among these three mouthpieces is both the cup depth and the rim width (subtracting the inside diameter from the outside diameter). The cup depth is not a factor yet since the cup on the visualizer has been removed. Rim width will affect the way the visualizer *feels* on your embouchure. Rim width also controls how well the visualizer seals on your embouchure and how much pressure it takes to achieve a good seal. The wider the rim, the better the seal with the least amount of pressure.

Refer to the Endsley Chart and do the following:

- Locate your present rim size along the far left column.
- Did the tip-up drill mentioned earlier achieve a nice full open sound on the buzz?
- If the answer was 'yes', you are probably playing on the correct size rim.
- If the answer was 'no', what did you see in the visualizer?
    - Lips weren't 50% – 50% or 60% (top lip) – 40% (bottom lip) inside the rim. *Reason* – rim may be too low on the embouchure.
    - I couldn't get any sound at all. The air could barely even get through the lips. *Reason* – biting the lips together, or the rim is too small (too much flesh inside the rim). If you are playing on a rim size between 8C and 2, you'll notice that the inside diameter on all of these mouthpieces is .655. If you want to try a larger inside diameter measurement you'll have to go to the 1 ½C or a .671 inside diameter measurement. All of the mouthpieces between 1 ½C and 1 have the .671 inside diameter measurement. If you think you need a smaller inside diameter measurement you'll need to try the 8 ½ to get an inside diameter measurement of .640. (Some jazz players go to the 10 ½ rim for the .624 inside diameter measurement.)
    - The visualizer is not in the middle of my embouchure. *Solution* – move it to the middle and see if that helps. Remember that the visualizer needs to be placed so that 50 – 60% of the upper lip is inside the rim.
    - I got a buzz, but the sound is really thin and airy. *Reason* – the rim is too big and you're biting together to keep control, or there is too much pressure on the top lip. Try a

slightly smaller rim size (the number) with the same inside diameter. If that doesn't achieve the sound you're looking for, try the smaller inside diameter with a smaller rim.

- I can see that I am playing with too much pressure on my embouchure. *Reason* – the rim may be too small or too rounded to achieve the proper seal to the embouchure. The visualizer rim must have the proper width and shape to achieve a good seal without too much pressure. After you feel comfortable with the rim size and inside diameter measurement, you should now try to vary the rim width. Many professional players can feel the difference between a .399 rim width (1 ½C) and a .409 rim width (1 ¼C). Many other players cannot feel much difference at all. This sensitivity is mostly due to the amount of hours spent playing the trumpet each day. Try several rim widths to determine whether you can feel the difference. If you have thin lips, you will need to be very careful about rim width due to the fact that thin lips cannot take very much pressure. I suggest that players with thin lips need to roll them in slightly to achieve a cushion on which to place the visualizer. Players with fleshy lips will not need to roll the lips in since the cushion already exists. However, many fleshy-lipped players like the feeling of a wider rim on the embouchure so that a good seal on the embouchure is achieved without too much pressure. Many mouthpiece manufacturers build a wide rim mouthpiece.

I don't have access to a visualizer yet. Can I go through this process with trumpet mouthpieces?

Yes, although it will not be as easy. In my opinion, trying to do this with a mouthpiece is less efficient and does not allow you to see what is actually happening inside the cup of the mouthpiece. However, if you need to do this without a visualizer, let's try this with your mouthpiece. Do this work in front of a mirror and in this order:

- Fit the rim size to your face by trying the mouthpiece you are currently using. Try that mouthpiece on your trumpet. If that mouthpiece achieves the sound you're listening for, you may be done.

- If not, go to your bag of mouthpieces (or borrow some from your trumpet buddies), use the same rim size (the number), and go one cup size deeper or one cup size shallower (refer to the Endsley chart).
- If this achieves the sound you're listening for, you may be done.
- If not, try another cup size deeper, and then try another cup size shallower.
- If you're still not satisfied, you may have selected the incorrect rim size to start with. Try one inside diameter size bigger, then one inside diameter size smaller to start with (refer to the Endsley Chart). Then, vary the cup depth as before.
- If this does not produce the desired sound, begin again with the interior rim size that feels best, and start varying the cup depth.
- The last thing to vary will be the width of the rim itself (rim width on Endsley Chart).

After I feel that I've selected the correct visualizer for the shape and size of my embouchure, what should I do next?

As I stated before, reflexes that are properly built for trumpet playing will decay over time and will need to be reinforced. It is my feeling that beginning each morning on the alto horn mouthpiece in front of a mirror and checking the buzz on a visualizer in the mirror provides daily reinforcement of the reflexes necessary for a great sound. There are mornings when the buzz will not respond the way we expect it to. Those are the days when we need a little more time on both the alto horn mouthpiece and the visualizer in order to achieve consistency.

After the buzz routines on the alto horn mouthpiece are completed, then proceed to the visualizer. (Stay in front of the mirror.)

Many mornings I start with the tip-up drill described on page 52 just to ensure that I am using the proper amount of weight on my embouchure and that the visualizer placement on the embouchure is correct. I then begin the drills in Appendix II.

Be sure to read the bulleted cues included with each step of the visualizer buzzing routine as a reminder of your goals in each section.

Try to start with the visualizer on middle C on the piano. Buzz a few long tones to connect the air intake to the air column as you blow. After a couple of long tones, proceed with the exercises in Appendix II.

You will notice that the goal range for the visualizer is much wider than it was for the alto horn mouthpiece, especially in the upper register.

Figure 43 The visualizer buzz range

Approach each fermata in Appendix II as a long tone. Hold the pitch steady and feel the air column as you blow in a consistent manner. Take a full deep breath after each fermata and continue in this manner to the end of each exercise. At the end of each exercise, pull the visualizer off of the embouchure and reset for the next exercise.

What should I look for when I'm playing the exercises on the visualizer?

When you start on the middle C (on the piano) you should see a fairly open and relaxed aperture. The aperture should extend across the inside diameter of the rim of the visualizer with at least 50% of the upper lip inside the rim (55 - 60% would be better). You will also start to notice that the angle of the visualizer to your face will change as you ascend. This is the beginning stage of the pivot motion explained in Unit 4 on page 17.

Many trumpet teachers refer to the ‘up air stream’ and ‘down air stream’ to explain how the direction changes as we move through the range of the trumpet. This change of air stream direction occurs inside the mouthpiece cup. I never thought about the concept much because I could not see it happening until I started working with the visualizer. With the cup of the mouthpiece removed, I could finally see the change in direction. I realized that the change in air stream direction correlated directly with the motion of the pivot. In Figure 44, notice that the angle of the visualizer is higher than in Figure 45. Figure 44, which shows the up air stream, produces a lower pitch.

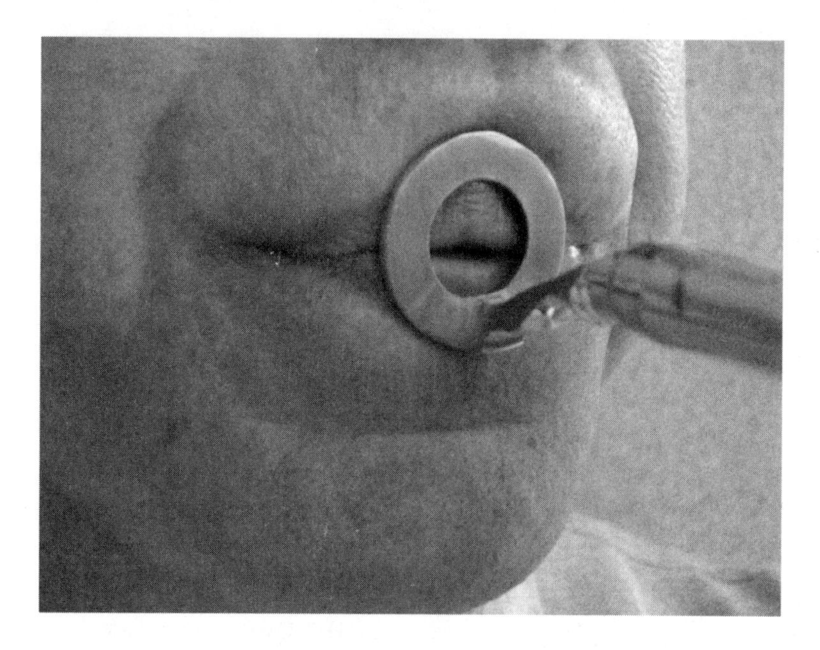

Figure 44 The up-air stream with the pivot

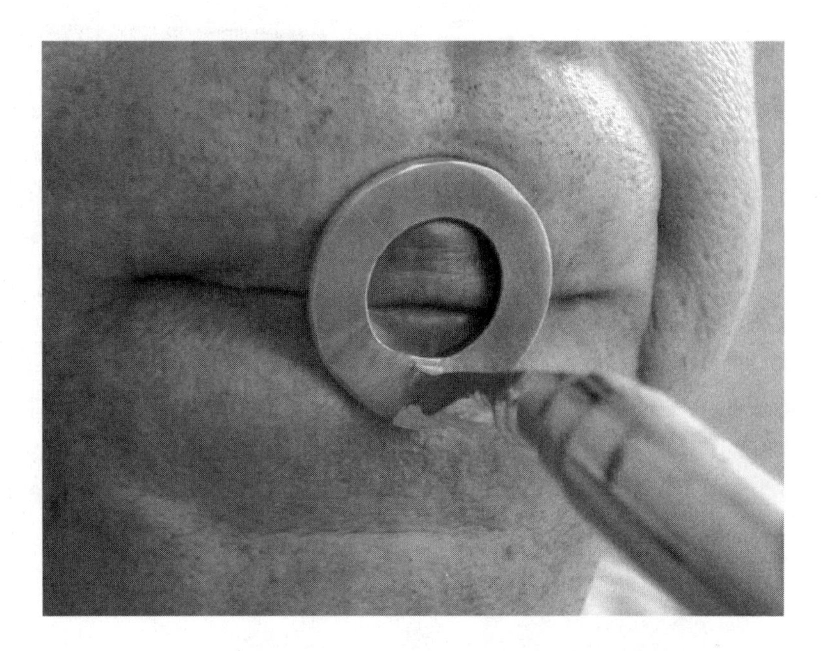

Figure 45 The down-air stream with the pivot

Now that you can see the change in direction, you can work on it every day.

What should I listen for while working on the visualizer?

In the beginning stages you should try to hold the aperture fairly open and relaxed. This embouchure position will achieve a relaxed buzz once the air stream is moving fast enough. Try to work toward a fairly loud full sound moving lots of air. *Do not try to play softly!* It is possible to play the middle C on the piano by not moving very much air, pinching the lips together and controlling the pitch by closing the throat. Try instead to take a full deep breath and blow it all out. Play forte. You will then be forced to relax the embouchure or a note much higher than middle C will be produced.

In addition, I like to hear some air actually going into the hole. With the cup removed (see Figure 46), you can see the hole.

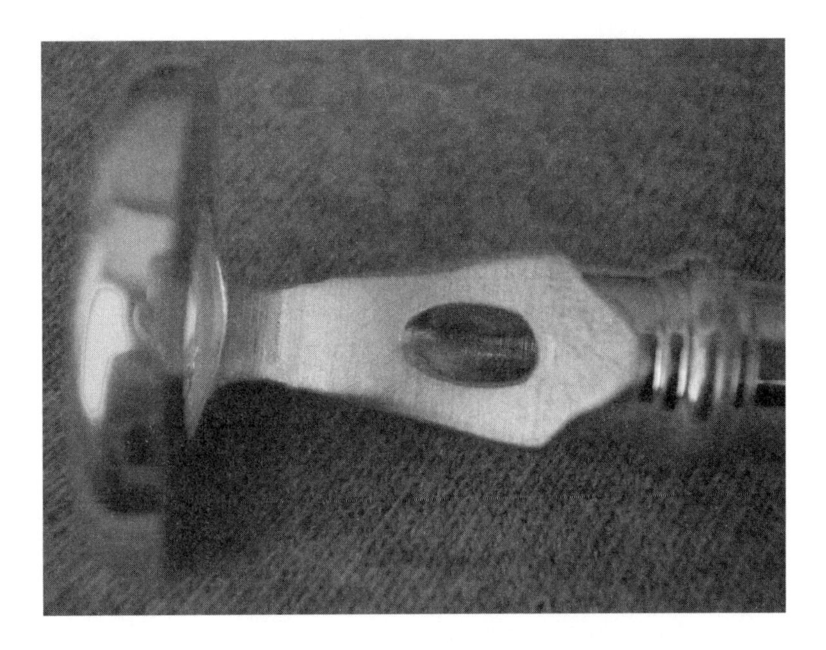

Figure 46 The visualizer hole

Focusing the air in this manner will give you more control of the air stream and you will be able to feel and to see the up/down air stream/pivot in action.

I'm not quite sure what to do in order to play higher on the visualizer.

Back in Unit 3 I talked about controlling air speed by leaving the throat open and blowing the air column through the mouth to the buzz. We can control the speed of the air by raising and lowering the tongue according to changes in vowel shape; oh, ah, eh, ih, ee.

As you ascend using the visualizer, you should start to work on the tongue height reflex group. Many players cannot feel this change in tongue height. The easiest way to explain this movement is by whistling. Do not move your lips as you whistle. Just move your tongue up and down.

Try this whistling exercise at the piano:

Figure 47 The whistling exercise

Now you can feel the tongue motion inside your mouth. Try to apply this feeling to the upper register of the visualizer.

When buzzing in the upper register of the visualizer you will also hear a change in tone quality. The sound of the buzz, which is wide and full in the lower range, becomes much more focused in the upper range. The sound becomes somewhat edgy or 'screechy'.

Try to ascend higher each day or two. When you reach a point where you can feel your throat starting to close, raise the tongue slightly and use a more closed vowel shape with the tongue. The vowels range from open to closed in this order: oh, ah, eh, ih, and ee. *Remember not to close the throat!*

When you first start using the visualizer as part of the daily warm-up, it may be fairly frustrating and might take some time to get used to. The time you spend on the visualizer may vary depending on the amount of success you experience. Just concentrate on the bulleted statements included with each exercise in Appendix II. *Remember, the visualizer is only a diagnostic and practice tool!*

Unit 13 The Mouthpiece

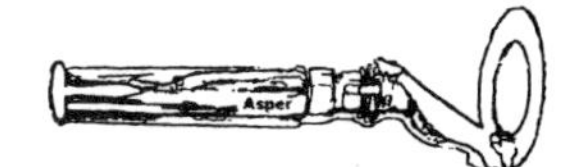

I've tried a variety of mouthpieces and I can *feel* a difference. What am I feeling?

You're feeling either the cup depth or the width of the rim (see Endsley Chart).

After inside diameter, cup depth is the next most important measurement to consider. The amount of volume inside the cup will have a major impact on the type of sound you will get on any mouthpiece. A deeper cup will allow more room for your lips to vibrate and will result in a darker, richer sound. You must achieve a balance between the mouthpiece (rim size, cup depth/shape, rim width), your embouchure shape, and the trumpet you are playing.

If you have thin lips, you will not need much room (inside diameter plus cup depth) for your lips to vibrate. In fact, if you pick a mouthpiece which has an inside diameter that is too wide and a cup that is too deep, you will not have the strength to hold the embouchure. Thin-lipped players can usually use a fairly average inside rim diameter (.655) and a slightly shallower cup.

Fleshy lipped players will need to use an inside measurement which is wider coupled with a cup depth which is fairly deep. This will give the fleshy lips more room to vibrate.

Remember, the statements I just made are pretty general and in the final analysis mouthpiece fitting is different for each player. It needs to be personalized. Do not pick a mouthpiece because someone else plays it. The mouthpiece needs to be fit to you! *Mouthpiece fitting needs to be controlled by your facial shape.*

You mentioned cup shape earlier. Where does that come in?

Several mouthpiece manufacturers are building cups that are shaped differently from the traditional bowl shape. There is a V cup, semi V cup, double cup, and many other variations of these. For the most part, these alternate bowl shapes are designed to produce a bright, highly focused sound. In this book, I am referring to the mouthpiece you will be using for orchestra, band, and solo playing. In these situations, you would want to achieve an open, rather dark orchestral sound. The 'traditional' bowl shaped cup is designed to produce this type of sound. If most of your playing would *not* be considered 'orchestral', you may then need a cup shape that is different than the 'traditional' bowl.

For example, when I'm called upon to play in an orchestral setting I play on a bowl shaped mouthpiece with a cup that is fairly deep. This combination, along with my trumpet, achieves the sound that I want to hear.

When I'm called upon to play in a brass quintet or a trumpet ensemble, I'll use a semi V cup for more brilliance and focus. If I'm playing jazz I may use a V cup for the most brilliance I can get from my trumpet.

So, you carry a bag of mouthpieces too! What makes your bag of mouthpieces any different from mine?

<u>They all have the same rim size</u>!

When I'm playing any of the mouthpieces in my bag, my face feels no difference. The rim is the same size and the rim width is the same. I am varying the cup depth and shape to achieve the sound that I want to hear, based upon the performance requirements.

In brass quintet or in jazz settings I may use different horns, or horns in different keys. Using the same rim size and rim width helps my consistency when moving from horn to horn. I don't have to alter my embouchure each time I change horns. I use the same rim size on piccolo trumpet that I do on the flugel horn.

How do I use the trumpet mouthpiece in the mouthpiece buzzing routine?

The exercises on the trumpet mouthpiece follow the exercises on the mouthpiece visualizer. As you read the bulleted statements in Appendix III, you'll see that many of them are the same as the statements applied to the visualizer. The biggest difference will be the sound that you are able to achieve on the mouthpiece with the cup attached. This sound should be big, wide and forte. The other goals that were applied to the visualizer *still apply here; breathing, relaxed buzz, embouchure symmetry and angle of the mouthpiece to the face.*

You will notice that the starting note for the trumpet mouthpiece, middle C on the piano, is the same as the visualizer. Continue watching yourself in the mirror. Pay particular attention to the bulleted statements.

Many players experience a drastic change in the sound they are able to produce on the trumpet mouthpiece. This is due to the prior work on the alto horn mouthpiece and the visualizer – in that order. The specific attention to the relaxed buzz is the reason for the change. Always work toward this open sound on the mouthpiece.

When I tongue on the visualizer and then apply that tonguing technique to the trumpet mouthpiece, it sounds like I'm tonguing way too hard. Is that normal?

Yes. Remember that one of our goals is to play with a more relaxed buzz (lower buzz pitch inside the cup of the mouthpiece). If this relaxation is actually taking place, then the tongue strike will not need to be as strong, heavy or hard. It will actually take less power from the tongue strike to get the buzz started since the lips inside the mouthpiece rim are being held in a more relaxed manner. *You will be able to tongue more gently!* This is especially true in the lower register of the trumpet mouthpiece or the trumpet.

What will my range goals be for the trumpet mouthpiece?

As you ascend through the range of the trumpet mouthpiece you will experience the same movement of the embouchure that you experienced using the visualizer. As you continue to ascend into the upper notes on the trumpet mouthpiece there will be an upper limit for each player. This upper limit is controlled by the shape of the mouthpiece, rim size, and, to a large extent, the shape of the embouchure. As you extend the trumpet mouthpiece range lower each day, there will be a lower limit that will finally be established. However, we should all strive to push the upper and lower limits of the mouthpiece buzz over time. I establish an upper and lower range goal for each warm-up. This three-octave range is included below.

Figure 48 The trumpet mouthpiece buzz range

Those players who play very efficiently in the upper register or those players who are either jazz lead players or are trying to become jazz lead players should explore the upper limits every day. Frankly, this upper limit varies from player to player. *Remember, every trumpet player cannot be made into a jazz lead player.* Most jazz lead players come by it very naturally and this ability to play in the extreme upper register usually occurs before college. Strides can be made with changes in equipment, but it is my strong belief that most jazz lead players were born with just the right facial structure to enable them to develop in that direction.

Why do you say that?

I know lead players with lip shapes varying from fleshy to thin. However, most players who have any kind of teardrop shaped lips have a harder time in the extreme upper register. This is due to the fact that the teardrop needs more room to vibrate, and since the teardrop is mostly flesh, the player has less control over it. Teardrop embouchures also need larger rim sizes to accommodate the extra lip mass. The larger rim sizes do not play in the extreme upper register very efficiently.

Players with fleshy or thin lips can both be successful in the extreme upper register. The fleshy-lipped player has more cushion, so they can use slightly more pressure on the embouchure. Thin-lipped players can play very efficiently using more muscle within a smaller rim. However, the thin-lipped player needs to play with less pressure on the embouchure.

How long will I spend on the trumpet mouthpiece each day?

The length of time spent on the trumpet mouthpiece will be quite consistent. After spending time on the alto horn mouthpiece and the visualizer each day, most players find that the response on the trumpet mouthpiece becomes very predictable. After the initial couple of weeks most players find that 5-7 minutes per day is enough.

You mentioned earlier that the angle of the visualizer would be important. When does this visualizer/trumpet mouthpiece angle apply?

After working with the mouthpiece visualizer for several weeks, most players begin to achieve an efficient buzz. They also find that the buzz efficiency is affected by the angle of the visualizer to the embouchure. When we are buzzing on the trumpet mouthpiece the angle must remain the same as it was with the visualizer. If it doesn't, we'll hear the difference in the sound that is produced. Changing the angle of the mouthpiece or the visualizer is really an adjustment we have called the *pivot*. Using the angle that we have established using the visualizer and the trumpet mouthpiece, we can now place the trumpet onto the mouthpiece at that same angle. This is quite difficult to do by yourself. Let me make a suggestion.

Once you have established the mouthpiece angle that is most efficient for you, get a friend to help you with the next step. With your friend holding your trumpet, take your trumpet mouthpiece and place it on your embouchure and buzz. After buzzing for a few seconds, stop blowing and freeze in place. Have your friend place your trumpet onto your mouthpiece. Now, look at the angle made between your *trumpet* and your face. Is this the angle you currently use?

Figure 49 Placing the trumpet at the correct horn angle

If the answer is yes, then you are already playing with an efficient horn angle in relation to your jaw and lip structure. You may then continue with the trumpet warm-up included in A Physical Approach to Playing the Trumpet, or the warm-up that you usually use. You may find, as many players do, that the time that you spend on the trumpet during the warm-up will be greatly reduced. Many days I need considerably less time on the trumpet before I continue my daily practice routine.

What should I do if my horn angle changed?

I would recommend that you continue the trumpet warm-up in front of the mirror. You now need to monitor the new horn angle. I would spend 5-10 minutes playing long tone exercises from A Physical Approach to Playing the Trumpet or from another exercise book. Do the long tones slowly while resetting the trumpet on the embouchure each time you change notes. Make sure that the new horn angle is consistent (taking pivot into consideration) as you ascend and descend through the range of the trumpet. *Continue to stay in front of the mirror throughout the long tone exercises!*

Once I have established the horn angle, am I done with the mouthpiece routine?

Yes, however, you may not be completely warmed up. I continue with a fairly short warm-up on the trumpet. I always start with long tones and stay in front of the mirror. If the warm-up has gone well so far, I may step away from the mirror. I continue with descending arpeggios into the pedal range and ascending arpeggios into the upper range.

I've never really had a consistent warm-up routine. Should I use one?

Yes. I have written extensively concerning the daily trumpet warm-up in A Physical Approach to Playing the Trumpet and believe that all trumpet players should use a consistent warm-up routine each day. A Mouthpiece Buzzing Routine for Trumpet simply adds more extensive mouthpiece buzzing to the beginning of the warm-up. Many players feel that the time spent on the mouthpieces 'warms them up' quite well before ever playing the trumpet. *Do not misunderstand; the buzzing routine is not a substitute for practicing!*

It is, instead, an efficient way to begin the warm-up each day without subjecting your embouchure to the weight of the horn at the beginning.

Conclusion

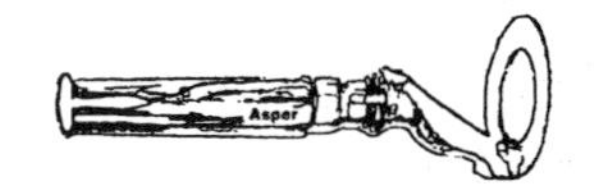

I have been using this buzzing routine for over a year now and have found that it has helped me greatly. It has been an interesting journey.

I have started my warm-up routine with trumpet mouthpiece buzzing for quite a long time and some days I could feel that something was not right. I had trouble pinpointing the problem when I just buzzed on the trumpet mouthpiece. I then had a visualizer built for me that had the same rim size as the trumpet mouthpiece I was playing. I quickly discovered that the mouthpiece rim that I was playing on was not efficient at all. I then built some visualizers myself and the experimentation began. Through this process, I eventually changed the rim size of all my mouthpieces.

I initially experienced some frustration with visualizer practice as I discovered inconsistency in my buzz from day to day. I could now see the inconsistency in the mirror every day and correct it. Over time, this new buzz consistency has translated into more consistency on the trumpet.

My first experience on the alto horn mouthpiece was interesting. I very much enjoyed the relaxation I felt right from the beginning. I discovered, however, that I did not always take a full breath before the buzz exercises – especially if my warm-up was early in the morning. After a week or so I was able to buzz up and down the range of the alto horn mouthpiece fairly easily. Standing in front of a mirror and watching my embouchure 'work' gave me an insight into what I should be looking for in the symmetry of my embouchure. This process seemed to also get my brain engaged to do the work of the day.

From the very first day I was surprised by the response of my embouchure on the trumpet mouthpiece after working on the alto horn mouthpiece and then the mouthpiece visualizer. The buzz responded correctly and with a bigger sound than I had achieved starting on the trumpet mouthpiece alone from the beginning of my buzz routine.

The biggest impact of the mouthpiece buzzing routine has been the amount of time I actually have to spend on the trumpet warming up each day. This time has been *greatly reduced.* I feel quite warmed up and ready to play after just a few arpeggios on the trumpet to double check that everything is working properly. *I can warm-up my embouchure each day without having to have the weight of the trumpet on my face.*

I hope that you are able to make good use of this book and find the right mouthpiece and buzzing routine for you.

“We are what we repeatedly do.
Excellence, then, is not an act, but a habit”

Aristotle

“Practice does NOT make perfect.
Only perfect practice makes perfect.”

Unknown

Appendix I Alto Horn Mouthpiece Buzzing

- Stand in front of a mirror.
- Hold the alto horn mouthpiece between the thumb and index finger of the left hand near the end of the mouthpiece.
- Place the alto horn mouthpiece in the middle of your embouchure and take a deep breath (Ho).
- Start buzzing on a relatively low note as in the first line of music on the opposite page (all pitches are on the piano).
- Watch the shape of your facial muscles.
- Keep the lips firm from the sides of the mouthpiece out to the corners of your mouth.
- Roll your bottom lip in slightly (for thin lips).
- Play f-ff and remember to pivot when moving between registers.
- Each line should be played as a separate exercise.
- Pull the mouthpiece off and rest after each line for as long as it took you to play the line.
- Try to expand your alto horn mouthpiece range each day until you can play all of the exercises.
- Extend your lower range down at the end of each descending scale to your lowest note.
- Try to buzz the low G, an octave and a fifth below middle C on the piano (bottom line in bass clef).
- The 4th line D in measure 27 may be close to the top of your buzz range.
- You should spend 5-7 minutes on this exercise each day at the beginning of your warm-up.
- On mornings after a heavy playing day, you may need to spend more than 7 minutes.
- Remember, you're trying for a big relaxed buzz using plenty of air!
- When you can play all of the exercises, write you own! (See Appendix IV)

Alto Horn Mouthpiece Buzzing

Appendix II Mouthpiece Visualizer Buzzing

- Stand in front of a mirror.
- Hold the visualizer between the thumb and index finger of the left hand near the end of the visualizer (hole on the bottom) so you can hear airflow into the hole at the bottom of the cup (which is gone).
- Place the visualizer on the middle of your embouchure with about 50% of each lip visible in the inside of the cup (a little more upper lip would be better, see Unit 8, page 34).
- Be sure to take a deep breath (Ho Breath).
- Start on middle C if you can. If not, start on any pitch and check it on the piano. Start the exercise there.
- Try to start lower each day!
- Watch the aperture in your buzz (between the lips). Keep the aperture as open and as relaxed as possible so it can buzz.
- Make sure that the aperture is even all of the way across the inside of the visualizer ring.
- You'll see an up air stream when you're buzzing low and a down air stream when you're buzzing high.
- Listen to the air go into the hole.
- Remember to pivot some to change the placement of the anchor. Get the open sound with the buzz.
- Pull the mouthpiece off and rest after each line for as long as it took you to play the line.
- Remember; play on one embouchure throughout the range.
- Try to extend your visualizer range each day until you can play all of the exercises.
- Extend your lower range down at the end of each descending scale to your lowest note.
- You should spend 5-7 minutes on this exercise each day after buzzing on the alto mouthpiece.
- Remember, you're trying for a big relaxed buzz using plenty of air!
- When you can play this page, write your own exercises! (See Appendix IV)

Mouthpiece Visualizer Buzzing

Appendix III Trumpet Mouthpiece Buzzing

- Stay in front of the mirror!
- Hold the trumpet mouthpiece between the thumb and index finger of the left hand near the end of the mouthpiece.
- Place the trumpet mouthpiece in the middle of your embouchure just as you did with the visualizer.
- Be sure to take a deep breath (Ho Breath).
- Start on middle C if you can. If not, start as low as you can.
- Watch your embouchure react as it did with the visualizer (lip firmness in embouchure).
- Pull the mouthpiece off and rest after each line for as long as it took you to play the line.
- Remember; do not change the embouchure throughout the range of the exercises.
- Try to extend your mouthpiece range each day until you can play all of the exercises.
- Extend your lower range down at the end of each descending scale to your lowest note.
- Try to buzz the low A, an octave and a minor third below middle C on the piano.
- Set an upper range goal of A, an octave and a major sixth above middle C (three octave range).
- You should spend 5-7 minutes on this exercise each day following the visualizer buzzing exercises.
- Remember, you're trying for a big relaxed buzz using plenty of air.
- When you can play this page, write your own exercises! (See Appendix IV)

Trumpet Mouthpiece Buzzing

Appendix IV Writing Your Own Exercises

Before you begin to write your own exercises, let me explain the reasons that Appendices I, II, and III were written using that specific melodic motion.

When we are practicing using the buzz, we want to practice the changes in embouchure firmness and amount of pivot gradually at first. You will notice that each exercise begins with scale wise motion. Using this motion will help us practice the gradual changes that need to take place in different registers of the trumpet. You will also notice that I do not introduce any interval greater than a second until the middle of each exercise (the interval of the 4th). Then the third part of each exercise begins with the interval of the 4th.

As you start to write, begin with longer lines that are mostly scale wise motion (see Exercise 1). Remember; do not use too many intervals at first. As you progress, start using more intervallic motion using arpeggios (major, minor, augmented and diminished). Refer to the other examples provided.

As your exercises get longer and longer, you may instead try playing some longer preexisting exercises. I like to use the Herbert L. Clark Technical Studies for the Cornet book. When using Clark remember to pick the keys that stay within the ranges for each mouthpiece/visualizer. Try to expand keys each day.

Some players like to warm-up on the trumpet using chromatic scales. Chromatic scale practice is an excellent way to see the pivot and to feel the gradual changes from a relaxed to a firm embouchure and the relaxed to firm buzz. You can achieve the same result by practicing this motion on all three mouthpieces using the glissando. Try a glissando within the ranges outlined on page 85 for each mouthpiece. If your sound breaks up, go to that pitch and try to discover which notes were affected. Then simply slur to and from the notes on either side of the affected notes. In essence 'massage the break'. After you feel confident that you have solved the problem with the buzz, try the glissando again.

Start each exercise on any pitch within the range for each mouthpiece/visualizer.

Range for the Alto Horn Mouthpiece

Range for the Visualizer

Range for the Trumpet Mouthpiece

Keep the intervals the same within each key.

Exercise 1

Exercise 2

Exercise 3

Exercise 4

Exercise 5

Exercise 6

Bibliography

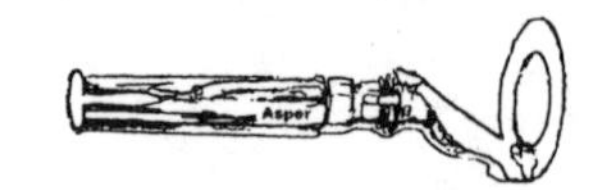

A PHYSICAL APPROACH TO PLAYING THE TRUMPET, by Lynn K. Asper. WaveSong Press: 1999

CLARK'S TECHNICAL STUDIES FOR THE CORNET, by Herbert L. Clark. Carl Fischer: 1934, second series, revised edition.

COMPARATIVE MOUTHPIECE GUIDE FOR TRUMPET, by Gerald Endsley. Tromba: 1992

WARM-UPS + STUDIES, by James Stamp. Editions Bim (Jean-Pierre Mathez): 1981, fifth edition.

Share the Mouthpiece Buzzing Routine with Others!

Do you know a trumpet player or teacher who could benefit from the unique ideas presented in A Mouthpiece Buzzing Routine for Trumpet? Spread the word!

Additional copies of A Mouthpiece Buzzing Routine for Trumpet are available in bookstores or directly from the publisher! To order, simply send $16.95 per book (Michigan residents add 6% sales tax) plus $4.00 postage and handling for one book (call or write for International Shipping and Handling), plus $1.50 for each additional book, to:

WaveSong Press
1138 Fairfield Dr.
Hudsonville, MI 49426

Include your mailing address and phone number along with your check or money order. Make your check payable to “WaveSong Press”. Quantity discounts are available. Contact us for details. Visit our website for other ordering information.

Phone: (616) 457-0562
E-mail: wavesong@att.net
Website: www.trumpetbook.com

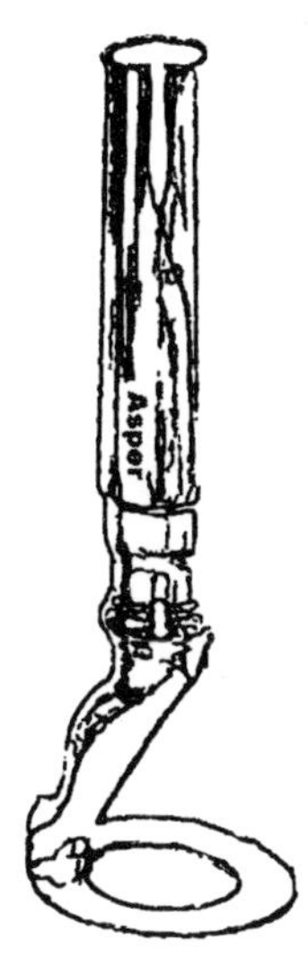

The Asper Trumpet Mouthpiece Visualizer

Available in sizes:
1c, 1¼c,1½ c, 3c, 5c, 7c, 10½c

Size really does matter!

Order Form

Name ______________________________

Address ______________________________

City ______________ State ______ Zip ______ Country ______________

E-Mail ______________ Phone # ( ) ______________

Quantity	Size	Cost @ $69.95 each
_____	_____	$________
_____	_____	$________
_____	_____	$________
_____	_____	$________
_____	_____	$________

6% MI sales Tax (if applicable) $________

Shipping @ $5.00 + $1.50 for each additional $________

(call or write for International Shipping and Handling)

Total # ________ Total $ ________

Mail check or money order to: WaveSong Press
1138 Fairfield Dr.
Hudsonville, MI 49426

Phone: (616) 457-0562